APPLAUSE FOR *CHARITY BASHED*

This frothy confection is equal parts glitter and grunge—a tabloid kingpin is murdered in Palm Beach and social worker Justine Romanoff descends into the decadent world of high-end philanthropy to solve the case…The prose is generally buoyant, reading like a catty gossip column of savage portraits of the sin-soaked elite [on] parade…Following a trail of embezzlement, vehicular fraud and blackmail, Justine discovers the lengths the latest wife of the victim would go to protect her reputation, and how far her employer would go to keep himself in a position to siphon off his charity's income…The novel is a solid effort and tight social drama that…sparkles.

—*Publishers Weekly*

Deliciously detailed and bitingly funny.

— @thewhinydonor, *Twitter*

Charity Bashed is full of outrageous scenarios and witty puns…*Charity Bashed* is the tabloid of mystery books.

—@ashleyhasty, *Instagram*

Salacious scoop…Ever wonder what really happens behind closed doors at the secretive, posh enclaves of Palm Beach society? Sharon Geltner knows.

—*Boca Raton Observer*

Janet Evanovich meets Dominick Dunne.

—Peter Rubie Literary Agency

Glitz and glam and murder. The lengths some will go to maintain their social status. I was glued to it. With laugh out loud funny parts. This was a delight. Don't miss it.

—Dawnny-Book Gypsy, *Goodreads*

Nicely written. Characters sparkly, sparky and engaging.

—@places_and_books, *Instagram*

D1566311

The old adage that writers write what they know about has never held more true than with Sharon Geltner...nobody is more qualified...to chronicle the lifestyles of the island's rich and famous...Terrific tale of murder, blackmail, selfishness and selflessness that it seems can only happen in Palm Beach 'who do you know?' circles.

Geltner begins *Charity Bashed* with these words: "My tiara's too tight." That's enough to get anyone interested from Palm Beach to Newport.

—Steve Pike, *The Coastal Star*

...Highly suggested reading. Geltner's style and humor fall in line with Florida Fiction favorites like Tim Dorsey, Carl Hiaasen and Dave Barry. *Charity Bashed* perfectly encapsulates the false reality of Palm Beach, describing standard Island hygiene as teeth whitening and Botox...Grab some macaroons, thrown on your tiara and read *Charity Bashed*. Or you can enjoy it like I did, on the beach in a bikini. Either way, it's Worth the read.

—@theflohemian, *Instagram*

Charity Bashed offers novel look at wealthy characters. [Readers are] exposed to the world of socialites and the moneyed class

—*South Florida Sun-Sentinel*

Hilarious and witty murder mystery featuring Justine, the "chief panhandler" for a charitable organization, she finds herself in the thick of things when a philanthropist winds up dead in the pool the day before a big shindig. Told in the first person, Justine's wry observations of those around her are hysterical, as well as the chapter headings ("Hope Floats, But Not Her Husband;" and "There's No Place Like Gnome"). The writing reminds me of a wittier entry in the Rachel Benjamin series, but this one...seems much funnier.

—Amazon Top Reviewer

Real page turner...her sense of humor will make you laugh out loud.

—Tim Byrd, *Palm Beach Live Work Play*

Charities aren't as fluffily-pure as they pretend to be. [This book is] fun...light-hearted, upbeat, humorous.

—@curiousbookreviewer, *Goodreads*

What a hoot this book was. The writing style and main character Justine Romanoff were reminiscent of Kinsey Milhone of Sue Grafton's ABC mystery series...I lived in an upscale community many years and Ms. Geltner has captured the residents of a posh enclave perfectly...In some ways it's like living on a movie set and you're waiting for someone to run in and yell CUT!!

—Barbara Khan, *Baer Books Blog*

Charity Bashed...was inspired by [author's] experiences raising money for Palm Beach charities. It's a fun murder mystery set in Palm Beach Island...The plot begins with a $10 million donor found dead in an oceanfront pool, following which a charity fundraiser stops "panhandling amongst the elite," and begins investigating fraud, mayhem, murder and relentless social climbing. All in that order.

—*Palm Beach Post* / Notables

Charity Bashed is a beach read...it's a satirical mystery amongst the island country club set in Palm Beach, and it's gotten rave reviews in *Publishers Weekly*.

—*Palm Beach Post* /Accent

Filled with larger-than-life and the occasional tiara-wearing characters, this was a fun, enjoyable adventure that I found myself cackling from chapter to chapter...

Justine's relatable sense of humor sparkles along with each page. Not a member of the Palm Beach rich and famous herself, she represents what the other 99% of the country would do in her situation. This is a perfect book for summer and would be an engaging read at the beach. I definitely recommend it for its witty banter and intriguing murder mystery.

—@readingdiary, *Instagram*

I put it in my beach bag...really enjoyed it! Quick witted, fun and loved the characters!!!! I wish I was brave enough to write a book.

—Marisa Gothie, RW Bookclub, *Facebook*

Charity Bashed is a fun and frivolous murder mystery set to the glamorous backdrop of Palm Beach in Florida and its wealthy charity donors…This book provides an insight into the world of socialites and fundraising. As the author has previous experience with this industry, there's a sense that much of the shenanigans in the novel are not all that devoid from reality…zappy one liners and dry wit… Punchy murder mystery…light escapism, ideally read on a beach holiday!

—@glenjenreads, *Instagram*

When a philanthropist is found floating dead in a socialite's swimming pool, hours before he was to be honored for a $10 million donation, the hypocrisy hits the fan…a humorous look at the characters who power the "racket," that is, the charity business on America's snobbiest resort island. Hint: altruism is low on the list if priorities. Justice is served, Palm Beach style.

—Mystery Writers Association (FL chapter)

Who doesn't want to know what goes on at secretive and posh enclaves as the Palm Beach Country Club?

Especially, following the Madoff scandal.

Well, former charity fundraiser Sharon Geltner…has a 'birds-eye' view from the inside, and has written an entertaining book inspired by her [fundraising] experiences [including] fashion shows and lunches at the Four Seasons…Geltner also collected Ferragamo handbags on Worth Avenue to auction off to Ladies Who Lunch.

—Shani McManus, *Jewish Journal*

I really enjoyed it. I am really skeptical when it comes to murder mysteries but I really liked *Charity Bashed* and Justine as the main character. It reminded me of the [ABC] TV series, *Revenge*, one of my all-time favorites! …Immense insight [into] all these charity and fundraising events.

—Shannon Theumer, RW Bookclub, *Facebook*

PRAISE FOR SHARON GELTNER'S
FLORIDA JOURNALISM

Sharon Geltner, fund-raiser for Jewish charities in Bernie Madoff's super-rich, super-savvy, piggy bank, Florida...[serves up] An insider's explanation of how this elite arrogant bunch were easy marks for a $65 billion con, thanks to perks, privilege and a sense of entitlement.

—Cindy Adams, *New York Post*

Showdown With The Countess

Boca Raton's high-society set is buzzing about the $22 million spat between the newspaper and the countess. The royal ruckus began when [reporter] Sharon Geltner penned a profile...the story of a woman who married a wealthy tool and die maker from Yonkers, New York, paid a shyster $20,000 for a title and then very publicly held herself out to be of nobility.

The alleged countess was not pleased. "I want these two people out," she declared. "The editor and the writer. They don't belong in Boca Raton." [She] announced that she had cut a dozen Boca Raton charities out of her will—a move that would cost them an estimated $22 million—and would not restore them unless the [newspaper] apologized."

—Howard Kurtz, *Washington Post*

Sharon Geltner [was] a newspaper reporter and magazine writer before she became a fundraiser and publicist for some top-notch Jewish charities in Palm Beach County...[Her] literary agent, Jane Dystel...says her book will "scrutinize the super-rich in their unguarded moments in the money trenches of the opulent island resort town offering both anthropological and financial insights into the privileges, perks, and senses of entitlement that made them susceptible to the biggest swindle in recent history."

Ouch!

For more dirt — um, "information" — visit Dystel.com.

—Shannon Donnelly, *Palm Beach Daily News*

COMING SOON

RED, WHITE & ROYAL BLUE
Washington thriller and historical novel

FIND THE AUTHOR

Instagram: @sharongeltner

Twitter: @charitybashed
@sharongeltner

Facebook: @charitybashed
@sharongeltnerportfolio

Amazon Author Page: sharongeltner

Muck Rack: sharongeltner

CONTACT

geltnerATcharitybashedDOTcom

CHARITY
BASHED

SHARON GELTNER

This novel is entirely a work of fiction. Although it contains incidental references to actual people and places, these references are used merely to lend the fiction a realistic setting. All other names, characters, places and incidents are the product of the author's imagination. Any resemblance to actual persons, living or dead, events or locales is entirely coincidental.

ISBN-13: 978-0991401345 Polo Publishing of Palm Beach
ISBN-10: 0991401344 Polo Publishing of Palm Beach

DEDICATION

In memory of my father, Bernard Benjamin Geltner,
who was an author in his own right.

"I did it my way."

CONTENTS

Chapter 1

MURDER IN PALM BEACH

"My tiara's too tight."

It wasn't the first time I heard that. I raise money for a charity, the Palm Beach Crisis Center. As chief panhandler for a nonprofit next to the richest island in the world, it's my job to help when jewelry weighs too much.

Mrs. Benjamin R. Ecklund's soft blond bangs were indeed flattened by her 400-carat gold and diamond coronet. I should have such problems.

"Mrs. Ecklund, you look magnificent," I said reassuringly. It was the truth. The Palm Beach socialite, who was going to host our charity gala tomorrow night in her oceanfront estate, was a stunner. Tiaras on women are like tuxedos on men. Anyone who donned one acquired a sudden regal elegance, often undeserved. Mrs. Ecklund had coronated herself.

Whoever said you can't buy class was wrong, especially here in south Florida. Not long ago, Brenda was a $23,000-a-year receptionist married to a mechanic at Tombstone Motorcycles in West Palm Beach. She ditched him to marry her elderly, yet frisky boss, one of the richest men in Palm Beach.

Sadly my powers of persuasion had fallen as flat as Mrs. Ecklund's hair. "The weight of all these jewels could crush my coiffure and ruin tomorrow night's publicity photos," she said.

I tried to look sweet and sincere. "You don't give yourself enough credit, Mrs. Ecklund. I guarantee in every shot, your updo will look fabulous."

Brenda Ecklund began to sparkle as brightly as her diadem. When she smiled, she seemed likeable. But the things that made her happy were sometimes a little scary, such as when Mrs. Ecklund got her hubby to cut his children from his previous marriages out of the will.

The junior Ecklunds' loss could be my employer's gain. Brenda wanted to be THE society matron of the island of Palm Beach and step number one, after snagging the spouse and bagging the house, was to host charity galas. That's why I was here begging for a cut of her dough. We sat in her tangerine velvet covered dressing room. It wasn't to my taste, but maybe the Bordello Tropicana stimulated her hubby.

How could I flatter Brenda into not making me run to Worth Avenue to borrow a new tiara at this late date? I had a million things to do before Brenda's shindig tomorrow night to honor Vincent Paul Louis, a Palm Beach VIP. He had pledged a huge donation to the Crisis Center to feed the poor, heal the sick, rehab his sleazy reputation, etc.

Brenda had cause to be nervous about her image. She'd donated a few hundred grand, money from her recent matrimony, or rather *matrimoney* to get the honor of hostessing our ball that required black tie and tiaras.

Brenda peered into the mirror. "Is there a scratch on this tiara?"

I went over for a closer look. "No, I don't think so."

Mrs. Ecklund asked, "Do you think my hair looks better up or down in my photos?"

"Hmmm," I said. "Well, down really shows off your eyes, but I think I prefer it up."

"Why?"

"Because it looks more queenly and you're going to be chairing this event, after all."

"I see what you mean," Mrs. Ecklund said. She nervously twisted her hair with her chubby fingers. Her 40-carat wedding rock, er, ring, glinted in the orange crush glow. I think what was bugging our little tangelo was all the Island galas and banquets were making her round as her favorite fruit. Mr. Ecklund found her pleasingly plump but Bootylicious Brenda did not want to burst out of her designer strapless mandarin satin gown.

Next to her septuagenarian husband, Brenda Ecklund looked like Viagra on a stick. She had pleasant, even features, nice smile, smooth complexion and pretty, thick, chemically enhanced ash blonde hair. Maybe Brenda hoped her figure wouldn't matter now that she was married and she'd be right—until the next clerk with cleavage came along.

I checked my agenda. I was supposed to suggest that Brenda get temporary lowlights to show off her gleaming gems and then segue into accessories. This could take another 45 minutes at least, but before I could get started on earrings, we were interrupted by a rapid succession of footsteps and ragged breath.

"Mrs. Ecklund?" a voice squeaked behind us.

We quickly turned from the ornate gilt mirror. It was Trisha Goulden, Brenda's Gal Friday. She was panting and leaning against the doorway. Usually Trisha was calm, cool and collected, bordering on wound too tight.

"What's wrong?" Mrs. Ecklund asked.

She seemed alarmed at Trisha's disheveled appearance.

"I wanted to tell you before the police came in."

"Tell me what? Didn't I already give to the annual Policeman's Fund?" Brenda sounded annoyed. She had often told me how irritating it is to live on the Island, as the locals call Palm Beach, because everyone has their hands out. No matter how much you give, they always want more.

"It never ends," Mrs. Ecklund had said.

But now Mrs. Ecklund said, "Send them around to the servants entrance." This was pretty considerate of her compared to other Island residents. When an on duty deputy sheriff arrived at the door of a local Campbell's Soup heiress, worth $900 million, she didn't answer.

"That is the duty of the household staff," Diana Strawbridge Wister later told the court. "I've never answered a door."

"The police aren't here to collect money," Trisha said. "They're here to collect evidence."

"Evidence?"

Brenda's moon face went blank. Her mouth puckered open.

3

I was baffled too. The two biggest cases in town in recent memory weren't all that intense. One involved an undercover operation to stop the sale of stolen designer handbags. The other was when a 225-pound antiques dealer assaulted a stripper, who was flirting with her husband at a surprise birthday at the Poinciana Club. But Brenda wasn't into fake Fendi, or fetching Fifi.

"They need the evidence for their criminal investigation."

"Investigation?" Brenda asked with disbelief and growing impatience. "You mean they aren't here to collect money for a new ambulance or fire truck?" The city often got its medical emergency and crime fighting equipment through random paternalistic donations from Island residents. Brenda and her Palm Beach neighbors lived on an Island with real estate valued at $5 billion but often didn't bother to lock their homes and cars. They treated town police like a private security force, even getting rides home when they got drunk.

Trisha said, "No, Mrs. Ecklund, the police aren't here to raise money for those new defibrillators."

"Then Trisha, what are they doing here?"

"Oh Mrs. Ecklund," Trisha said tearfully, "They found a dead man floating in your swimming pool!"

Chapter 2

ISLAND CRIME SCENE

A shocked silence followed as Brenda and I gaped at Trisha. Somehow I couldn't picture yellow crime scene tape wrapped around 40-foot tall royal palms on Brenda's fabulous pool side deck fronting the glittering Atlantic.

"Someone fell in the pool?" I asked.

Brenda glared at me for speaking.

"What the hell happened here?" She demanded to know.

"It's horrible. The police are recovering the body . . ." Trisha said with a wail.

"The Body?" Brenda screamed. The tiara tumbled from her head to the floor.

"The police are fishing out Vincent Paul Louis. There's crime scene tape everywhere."

Vincent Louis was the very same tycoon who was to be named Humanitarian of the Year at the gala Brenda was to chair at her home the following night. Vincent Paul Louis was the zillionaire who founded the trashy tabloid, the *National Intruder*.

As my mouth hung open, the gears began whirring. First of all, what was Louis doing at Brenda's home a day early? I thought it was a little soon for Brenda to be cuckholding her husband, who was as rich as Louis was, anyway. There was no money in it for her.

And if Louis was here for legitimate reasons and not an affair, why had he gone for a swim here, when his own Olympic-size pool was at his estate next door? Was he just out strolling when he suddenly felt ill and then toppled into the pool?

And why were the police called so quickly? Old men on dozens of medications keeled over on the Island all the time. Some say it's the heat, but I contend it's the humidity.

A petty thought occurred to me. Couldn't this have happened AFTER the soiree? The Palm Beach Crisis Center finally snagged the giganto donor it needed for 50 years and now it looked like our white knight dropped dead of a heart attack the day before he signed our check for $10 million?

"What happened?" Brenda asked.

Even in the radiantly orange room, she had gone as white as a frozen coconut daiquiri. Last month's elegant publicity photos had dropped to the floor in a heap by her pedicured feet.

"Mr. Louis drowned," Trisha said, starting to cry.

Like me, Trisha was a glorified servant, fulfilling the whims of the rich. Trisha counseled Brenda on purchases of art and wine and bathroom accessories. Brenda had once authorized her 10 hours' pay to find the perfect trash bin for under the kitchen sink—which Trisha did in 15 minutes at Bed, Bath & Beyond. Trisha was scared Brenda was going to shoot the messenger and then we'd have two dead bodies.

I ran to the cantaloupe-colored bathroom with its golden cherubs and got Brenda a glass of water. She probably needed something stronger, but I had no idea where she kept the Grand Marnier. Brenda looked dazed. Her hands trembled as she took the Waterford goblet I offered.

"How could this happen?" she muttered to no one in particular.

"Trisha, what's going on?" I asked.

Brenda hadn't heard. She stared into her now empty glass. "Why would Vincent kill himself?" she asked.

Suicide. I hadn't considered that option. Louis hadn't appeared distraught when I saw him recently. From what I heard he was a 'no regrets' kind of guy, as one might expect from a man who had started his paper on Mob money and ruthlessly blackmailed hundreds of celebrities over the decades.

Plus, why would he choose the Ecklunds' pool to do the dirty deed? So his wife wouldn't have to clean up after him? Considerate. But isn't that what maids were for?

"He didn't kill himself," Trisha said. "Mr. Louis was murdered."

We stared.

She added in a rush, "It happened about an hour ago the police think. The landscaping crew had finished the grounds by the lake and found him when they went out back by the ocean. They hadn't heard anything because of their electric hedgers."

I had never heard of a murder on Ocean Avenue, the ritzy boulevard lined with gigantic mansions. Jewel theft, yes. Drunken revelry, naturally. The occasional Kennedy accused of rape? I'm afraid so. But murder? Never. And one taking place while I was on the premises? I was chilled.

"How can you be so sure it was murder?" Brenda asked and handed me her glass for a refill. "Maybe it was an accident?"

"It was no accident," Trisha insisted and looked like she was going to be sick. "Before Mr. Louis drowned, his head was bashed in. Then he must have been pushed into the pool."

Then our communing was over. Mrs. Ecklund closed ranks. After all, though we could discuss tiaras and coiffures, and I was right there in her time of need, in the end, I was not on her payroll, which made me an outsider.

Mrs. Ecklund shook herself slowly as she accepted the refilled water goblet from me. She sat up straighter as she got control of herself and waved me away regally with her Cheeto orange nails.

"Justine, you may go."

Dismissed, just as things were getting interesting.

Chapter 3

HOPE FLOATS, BUT NOT HER HUSBAND

I had met the victim once around Thanksgiving, a couple weeks ago. It was strange to think of ruthless Vincent Paul Louis as anyone's "victim." I was at his estate to interview Louis and his Popsicle wife Hope for a laudatory press release with equally flattering photos for the *Shiny Sheet* about their big upcoming donation to the Palm Beach Crisis Center.

At the interview, Mr. Louis was shy at first, then nice enough when I went to their splendid manse for the photo op. His wife was a real witch. He shook my hand, while she eyed me coldly up and down. I guess he was under no illusions as to her true character, if he cared.

Over the years, Hope had smoothed the Tab King's rough edges. Despite Vinny's old time disreputable pals with Italian last names, the Louis's had climbed the social pinnacle through the time honored charity racket. They bought respectability with noisy, showy philanthropy. The couple even published their own newsletter telling the world how generous they were. It was full of glossy, color photos of the two at their various charity benefits. Unlike some of the Island's other society matrons, Hope Louis owned her tiaras.

Being the wife of a trashy tabloid publisher, Hope was understandably paranoid about my prying into her life and any possible hint of bad publicity. She glowered when I took notes. She glared when I loaded my camera with film as if I were loading bullets into a gun. However, she did dress up for the photo shoot. She had medals of dubious provenance pinned to her breast, and best of all, had donned a photogenic tiara. She looked magnificent.

Hope's face had been lifted five times, she had a recent eye job and her teeth were capped—all standard Island hygiene. It was said she was one of the few women in Palm Beach who hadn't had bodywork, except for her chest. Lady Bountiful attributed her slenderness not to lipo but to daily runs on the beach in front of her piazza. Her hair was different too. Instead of the usual helmut head, or Glenda Good Witch of the North shoulder length curls and swirls that her peers favored in the same shade of Billionaire Blonde, Hope's hair was bleached platinum and yanked back into a severe chignon. Her lips were scarlet. All she needed was a riding crop to complete the dominatrix look.

Mr. Louis lit a cigar and sat back in his antique, Hepplewhite wing-backed chair. I heard that, in front of company, he used to kick off his shoes and place his gnarled bare feet on the coffee table. This time he played the classy gent. However, even iron-willed Hope couldn't break him of his chain smoking habit that had blackened the newsroom of the *National Intruder* and had probably given lung cancer to countless employees.

"So, Mr. Louis, I know there's a lot of competition, but in all the time you ran the *Intruder*, what was your favorite story?"

He'd grinned. "It would have to be 'Headless Woman In Topless Bar.'"

I laughed. Donna Shaughnessy, *Shiny Sheet* "Society Editor" and my pal, would love that line! Even icicle Hope would thaw a bit when she saw the flattering coverage that would ensue from my efforts.

"But then, I never met a UFO, two-headed baby, Bermuda Triangle, Jeanne Dixon psychic prediction or Elvis sighting that I didn't like," Mr. Louis continued. "Those put plenty of bread on the table."

"But in later years the paper got much more serious about its coverage."

"Damn straight," Mr. Louis agreed. "We used to be reporting

pariahs. Let me tell you, little girl, I laughed all the way to the bank despite sniveling about how we brought down the standards of journalism. Today, every last one of them is at our level."

Mr. Louis began a lecture, "My top editor comes from Harvard. My reporters are from the *Washington Post* and other so-called legitimate papers. I'm interviewed on FOX and CNN about the news we break about prostitutes and presidents. Look how everyone followed us on local boy Rush Limbaugh's drug abuse, Jesse Jackson's love child, Clinton's Pardon Gate, Robert Blake's murdered wife and Chandra Levy's affair with a Congressman. Ever since the O.J. Simpson trial everyone has copied us. People and US have just put a slick cover on *Intruder* stories."

Since starting the gore-spattered *Intruder* in the fifties, Louis had influenced journalism worldwide, including Fleet Street. Ritzy Palm Beach County seemed to spawn tabloids. It was home to the *National Enquirer, Sun, Globe, National Examiner, Weekly World News*, the *National Intruder* being the most lurid and wackiest of them all. Where else in America can you say that and who else would want to?

"Critics have said that the *Intruder* is 'the Las Vegas of journalism.' Supposedly it 'was built on dirty money and bad taste.'"

Hope disliked her husband's candor. Like so many Palm Beach matrons, the source of the family fortune was a source of shame. But no one scorned the "Listerine heiress," or the "Kleenex" heirs. Cold cash smoothes away any awkwardness.

Hope snuggled her Lhasa Apso to her perhaps real breasts. The woman was a canine fanatic, but at least I didn't have to deal with her nerve wracking Chihuahua.

I took their photos by the massive fireplace flanked by two huge Christmas designer-decorated trees. Security-minded Hope would not allow me to shoot her and hubby in front of any of their oil paintings or other precious collectibles, which could invite theft. Mr. Louis insisted I shoot them in front of a photo of him with the Pope. I also shot them in front of the spectacular trees; full of shining ornaments Hope claimed "have been in our family forever."

Not all of them. Maybe it was my fevered imagination, but I could have sworn tucked near a wooden sleigh sprinkled with "snow" was an incongruous little blonde beauty pageant figurine in pink bathing suit. What an ego on that woman.

Then Mr. Louis had an idea.

"Honey, now that you've fired that girl, you're looking for someone new to edit that newsletter of yours. How about Justine, here? She's a twofer. She can write and take photos."

See what a bargain I am? I heard Hope not only looked like Eva Peron, but acted like her as well. She was a dictatorette who terrified her staff but paid well, especially by Florida standards, which are to the south of Mississippi's.

The society matron eyed me as coldly as a prison matron.

"Sixty-five thousand dollars is a lot of money for someone like you."

Mr. Louis winced. So did I, on the inside. Then, without a single feature moving on Hope's plastique face, a wall slammed shut behind her eyes and her upper lip seemed to sneer slightly. Did her pert little pig snout wrinkle? There was no goodbye, no farewell. There was no friendly shake of the hands. I had been dismissed.

Donna, my pal at the *Shiny Sheet* later clued me in, after she'd been to a holiday party at the Louis's. Just a single one of the five Xmas trees Hope displayed in her home cost $65,000.

Remembering all that, it was a shame that Hope was the Louis left alive.

Chapter 4

THERE'S NO PLACE LIKE GNOME

*O*nce I was alone and didn't have to put up a front, I felt shaken that someone I knew had been violently murdered with me nearby. I kept roaming my apartment, making sure everything was locked tight. I must have checked the dowel in the patio sliding door ten times.

I was too jumpy to read the copy of *National Intruder* I had bought as a gag. With what I knew about the murder, TV news seemed too scary.

I knew I would feel better if I called Donna. We had known each other for years, since working together at the daily newspaper, the *Shiny Sheet*, until my fall from grace. I blamed the *Shiny Sheet* for insidiously transforming me from cynical journalist to socialite wannabe.

Were those footsteps outside? I turned out the lights and peered outside. It was just Dan from across the street, walking the dog. I heard something outside. I turned out the lights and went to the back door, peering out between the blinds. The neighbor's cat was trotting across the top of the fence and something had fallen off. I was still jittery. I stopped pacing and went back to the phone. Besides being the Island's expert on faked genealogical, charitable and social resumes, Donna was an heiress, who summered in Martha's Vineyard. She knew where all the bodies were buried, or floated.

I was sure she was working late tonight on the Louis murder. I rang the *Shiny Sheet* newsroom, the epicenter being the Society desk.

"Society," Donna barked into the phone, like she always did. Donna didn't need to say anything refined. On the Island, hers was the ultimate greeting.

"Donna, it's me."

"Are you holding up OK?"

"Of course," I said, adding, "Are you working on the Louis case?"

"Yep."

Hmmmm, Donna wasn't usually circumspect with me. My antennae were on full alert. Because of the notoriety of the victim, this case would be national news.

"Donna, don't keep me in suspense," I said. "You know I was there this afternoon?"

"Yeah, I heard."

"And?"

Finally she came across.

"I know what the murder weapon was."

"No way!" I screeched. This reporter had impeccable resources, from the Hamptons to Lyford Cay.

"A garden gnome."

"A guardian what?" I asked, confused.

"A gnome, a garden gnome," Donna repeated, with less patience.

"I heard Louis' head got bashed in," I said, "but by a decorative poolside object?"

"Believe it. It was a bronze statuette of a gnome. It supposedly had a floppy night cap and pointy shoes that curled at the toes. Very kitsch."

"Bizarre."

How heavy was this gnome? And why hadn't Vincent seen it coming? Had his back been turned, while the killer awaited his chance to smash and run?

"One more thing, Justine," Donna said. "The police are going to question you soon."

"I figured," I said.

"Don't let on you know about the murder weapon. No one is supposed to know."

I paused and then asked, "Who did it?"

"I don't know, but neither do the police. Who do you think?"

If Donna's asking me she must be desperate. "Take your pick, Donna. He had hundreds of *Intruder* victims."

"I'm checking the local angles first," Donna said.

"You think his wife did it?" I really hoped Hope had. I'd love to see her behind bars, the kind without any liquor.

"Justine, how unkind," Donna said as she heard the eagerness in my voice.

"Tell someone who cares," I said coldly.

"The police have ruled out suicide . . . "

"No shit, Sherlock."

" . . . and robbery."

"How come?"

"The cops pulled Louis' wallet out of his pants pocket, and the $5,600 inside were dripping wet."

"Who carries that kind of cash?" I asked.

"In Palm Beach? Everyone."

"Do you think maybe it was a disgruntled employee, like one of his tab reporters?"

Donna briefly considered the question, but answered negatively. "No."

"Seriously, what about an indentured household servant who finally cracked?" Not that it was going to be as easy to investigate the serfs anymore. From 1940 to 1985, the town had fingerprinted and photographed all blue-collar staff and if any were caught without special ID, they were fined or thrown in jail.

Donna ignored my theories. "Did you hear anything today? See anything?"

"You know I hadn't or I would have told you!"

"I know, but I had to ask," Donna said. "I've been hearing rumors it might have been one of his mistresses."

"I didn't know he had one." But it figures, with the man/woman ratio in Palm Beach that guy, even in his late seventies, had to spread himself around. Plus, if Frostbite Hope were as icy in bed as she was in the drawing room, Vincent had risked freezer burn.

"I hadn't considered the sex angle . . . " I said.

"Well, you're the only one who hasn't," Donna responded, adding, "The police are also trying to dredge up Louis' old Mafia connections. Maybe an unpaid debt, family honor besmirched, I don't know."

I snickered. "Any racehorses?"

She said, "I'm serious. Vincent may have offended one celebrity too many."

I got serious too. "Donna? Do you think Island police are up to this?" "We're talking a capital crime and these guys drive home drunks and stop strangers for bald tires and expired license tags." The power dynamic was a tad uneven between the resort residents and their sworn protectors. The police did not have a union and starting pay was $40,000.

Donna agreed, "It's not like Island has a lot of practice investigating murders. I looked it up; guess how many there have been in the past 20 years?"

I was clueless. I hadn't heard of too many.

"Only 11." Donna explained most of them were easily solved because in Palm Beach, murders, like money, tend to stay in the family. The last real whodunit was in 1996, when a restaurateur surprised a burglar at home and was strangled to death. The killer, who had inspected her home for termites six months before, was caught soon after he tried pawning the victim's bracelet.

"How do you think Hope will take all this snooping?" I asked. "Intruding minds want to know."

Donna said, "Whatever Hope feels, when she does her star turn at the funeral, she will be wearing a flawless little mourning outfit, with tasteful, yet expensive, jewels."

"They're tasteful because they are expensive," I said.

We said goodbye and vowed to share any news we heard.

Chapter 5

OFFICE GOSSIP AT YENTA CENTRAL

There's nothing like a good murder to get me out of bed in the morning. I dashed outside to see what the paper had to say about Vincent Louis, the departed Tabloid King. I was hoping for a lurid front-page story, but instead I found the Island's latest corpse buried somewhere inside the back page. I'd seen jaywalking get more coverage.

I knew the police wouldn't disclose the head injury. But I didn't know Hope would have such success at suppressing the story. Unwanted media attention was even more of a nightmare for her than someone showing up at the same function wearing the same dress as she.

I tossed the paper onto my front step and mused about the murder. Instead of being out and about on this sunny morning I would be entombed at the office and working on my Florida pallor. As I dragged last night's garbage to the curb, I saw my next door neighbor doing the same, only with a lot more panache. Debbie wore a stylish new pastel yellow Egyptian cotton robe. I hurried over to compliment her on it, and share the news.

Debbie's husband is a Palm Beach garbage collector who, four times a week, finds amazing treasures in Island garbage cans. We neighbors called her "Debbie Dior," for the nearly new designer clothes her scavenging spouse snags.

"Did you hear the news?" I asked.

"I guess not," Debbie yawned and came up to talk. I approved the matching sash, scalloped hem and deep cuffs on the sleeves.

"Nice robe, Deb."

"Thanks," she proudly picked a nonexistent piece of lint off her lapel. "Dan never lets me down."

"He's quite the personal shopper," I said and then got back to business. "Debbie, don't tell me you didn't know. Vincent Louis, the Tabloid King, is dead."

Debbie looked shocked. "How?" She actually subscribed to many of the Tab King's publications, whereas I just picked them up on impulse in the checkout line. That made me intellectually superior.

"He drowned," I said.

"What? When?"

"Last yesterday afternoon. In his next door neighbor's swimming pool." I left out the part about how close I was to the murder scene. In my line of work, I didn't need the gossip. Notoriety is only useful for the Paris Hiltons of the world, meaning you should already be very rich and/or famous.

"I wonder how Louis' own papers will cover his passing?" Debbie asked. I hadn't thought of that. Louis' staff may be breaking out the Cliquot, but his papers would be draped in black.

She looked up at me and asked, "Didn't you tell me you guys were going to honor him soon?"

"Yes, he was going to give us $10 million."

"You'll still get it, right?" she asked, "You must be in his will."

"I hope so," I said, not really sure.

"Well Justine, no matter what, at least you got Dan and me to donate our Chevy Cavalier to the Palm Beach Crisis Center."

Uh oh. Was she hinting? Our office was sometimes late with thank you letters. I asked, "I really appreciate that—have we thanked you yet in writing?"

"Not yet," Debbie Dior said. "I'm sure we'll hear from you guys soon."

That was embarrassing, but Debbie mercifully changed the subject. We agreed to hit Boynton Beach Mall later that week to scout for items that Dan never found in Palm Beach such as thick-soled work shoes and gardening gloves. We said goodbyes and I headed inside to get ready for work.

I tossed the newspaper at my front door. I would have to rely on that old standby, my office. Rumor, innuendo, supposition, rank lies, the basest gossip . . . all of it saturated our workplace. And never before this morning was it more welcome.

I was pouring my usual five tablespoons of Florida-grown sugar into my coffee when Felicia Harold strode into my cramped, windowless office. "Spill your guts!" she ordered. "What do you know about the Louis murder?"

I hesitated. Felicia was a tricky customer. Her gossip skills were flawless, which was useful, but she often pumped me for information on our boss. I didn't know if it was because he was a target of some love campaign of hers, or she was a hopeless yenta. I was dying to learn what she knew about Louis, but then I'd have to admit I was near the scene of the crime. I didn't want that getting around the office.

Like me, Felicia raised money for the Palm Beach Crisis Center. Unlike me, she had a rich Daddy and society connections. Before working here she had been an accountant who embezzled hundreds of thousands of dollars from the family firm, spending it along Worth Avenue on the usual Palm Beach necessities, including oversized ruby-encrusted brooches in the shape of hibiscus blossoms and $9,500 lime green alligator handbags with jeweled clasps. She also bought climactically inappropriate wares such as fur-lined boots, sable coats, ski wear. Felicia was insatiable.

Her father caught on—maybe it was the mink-lined anorak that did it—and demanded that she stop. Felicia denied stealing and her father turned her in. However, her mother retained a high priced lawyer, who got Felicia off by pleading the novel, yet debilitating, "compulsive shopping disorder," otherwise known as "shopaholism." This being Palm Beach County, the judge fell for it. The County sentenced her to community service, which meant working at the Palm Beach Crisis Center.

It's not the first time a local judge saved the rich from themselves. The kept mistress of Palm Beach commodities trader and hospital philanthropist Marvin Schur left their two-year-old son alone in her million dollar home. As she bought a $350 birthday present on Worth Avenue, her son wandered into the unfenced pool and drowned.

Dora Chong faced between 13 and 30 years in prison but in a hush-hush hearing got off with 1,000 hours of community service. She later illegally fled the country.

When Felicia Harold cheated jail she got to choose between sorting clothes at the Salvation Army or sorting files for us. Soon after coming to the Crisis Center Felicia hit on an idea to attract donations.

"What you need to do is offer social services that benefit the wealthy," Felicia had suggested. "Why else would they help you?" She had gotten her mother to pay the Crisis Center $5,000 to start a support group for the affluent, led once a week by a therapist with four graduate degrees.

I finally answered Felicia. "Yes, I heard about the Louis murder. Scary, isn't it?" I thought again of how Vincent Louis had drowned after his head was beaten to a bloody pulp. It frightened and fascinated me at the same time.

"Scary?" she wailed, "It's terrible. He pledged us $10 million. Pledged, as in, we never got a check!"

That Felicia had the right perspective. Palm Beach's best kept secret was that multi-millionaires sometimes renege on their lush promises to impoverished charities. Elsewhere, a seduced, abandoned and then disgusted nonprofit would sue, but never in Palm Beach. When all is said and done, the Island is a very small town. One does not go public with one's complaints here, especially when your opponent can buy every ambulance chaser in the state.

"There's no way Hope will give to us now," she said.

"Well Felicia, we both know that giving to the wrong cause can be a deadly social faux pas." Had I really said "deadly?"

Somehow, I got the feeling it was not the snobby socialite's idea to help a declasse, most un-sexy social service agency such as our friendly neighborhood crisis center. Hope Louis was more into receptions and galas at theatres, museums, opera houses. She liked the kind of parties that gave away goodie bags with hand dipped chocolate truffles, perfume samples and certificates for free facials and massages. She liked parties where celebrities and actors roamed, not shabby shindigs that raised money to stock soup kitchens, school supplies and libraries.

Felicia tossed a foot high stack of newspapers off my guest chair and plopped down. I glanced over at her black shoes with thick leather straps crisscrossed up to her shins. Were those the new Dior bondage shoes? Delicious. She must have found herself a boyfriend. But how could she afford . . . ?

A boyfriend? And the shoes?

He must be into S&M, hmmmmm. Well, who isn't these days? At least that's what I heard. I wouldn't know.

Felicia shot a pained look at my pigsty of an office, the sloppiest amongst our 250 employees. Since I was incredibly productive in getting free press for the Palm Beach Crisis Center, saving it hundreds of thousands of dollars a year on advertising, I got away with it. Plus, I never met with donors in my office.

Felicia crossed her long, thin legs—her best feature. I sensed something calculating behind those carefully mascaraed eyes. Felicia's face always looked a bit hard with marionette thin lines going from her mouth to her nose. This was probably why she focused on her short skirts and sexy shoes.

"You would think Hope would come through for us after all we've done for her mother," she said with disgust.

We both knew better.

Palm Beach charities keep special locked file rooms for "high profile clients." The agencies that fund us demand special treatment for their biggest donors and their relatives. Our social workers were kind to all of their clients but the suits assumed only VIPs were treated well.

From these "secure" files, I knew Hope attended the Support Group for the Wealthy. We also knew that Hope had hired our geriatric social workers to check on her elderly mother, a retired seamstress from Akron, who was in the early stages of senile dementia.

"Hope will never acknowledge her debt to us because then her friends would find out," Felicia said.

"They'll find out her mother has Alzheimer's?" I hadn't known Hope was bothered by the stigma of mental illness.

"They'll find out her mother had to work for a living," Felicia said.

On the Island that was a bigger stigma. What Truman said about friendship and Washington, D. C. applies to Palm Beach too—if you want gratitude, buy a dog.

"Hope may not give to anyone," Felicia said.

"She has to give to someone," I said. "I heard the Louis' were planning to sell the *Intruder*. If Hope goes through with it, then she's going to need a serious tax break. You know as well as I, in her bracket, tax implications make it costly for her NOT to give to charity."

"It's true the IRS spurs a lot of Island altruism, but if Hope gives to anything," Felicia said, "then it's going to be the only thing that brings out her humanity."

"What's that?"

"Animals."

"What about her husband's legacy?" I asked.

"What legacy? 'Headless Woman Found in Topless Bar!' His

Mafia pals? Hope doesn't want anything to do with those parts of her husband's life." Felicia paused and then said, "I'm surprised she's bothering with a funeral."

"What?" I asked.

"We're just rolling into the height of Season. Grieving widowhood is really going to cramp Hope's style. Maybe she'll put Vince on ice until Easter."

We laughed. Felicia reminded me about the Islander who died at an inconvenient time, the social Season. The Italian aristocrat and real estate tycoon had died at age 90, leaving his 57-year-old widow with $300 million, but no escort. Burial was not an option. Instead, three days after he died, she hosted a blowout at the Biltmore. The funeral home chilled his embalmed bod for 40 days, until she could pencil him in.

"Well, whatever merry widow Hope plans to do, I'm sure she will be the chic-est mourner at the funeral," I said. "Maybe she'll wear shoes just like yours."

Felicia winked.

Chapter 6

WE PUT THE VILE IN SERVILE

*A*fter Felicia strutted out of my office wearing her five-inch heels, I had another visitor. Lucette from book keeping stopped by with her breakfast Coke. After a healthy swig, she wiped her mouth with the back of her hand and asked, "Do you think Pete will be at the funeral?"

Peter Pignatelli was never far from his employees' thoughts and fears, since he was top dog and dictator at the Palm Beach Crisis Center. Our agency motto was, "We are as dysfunctional as the families we serve." Or is that our mission statement?

"Not only will Pete be at the funeral, but I bet he'll do a eulogy," I predicted. We both looked over our shoulders to make sure no one overheard. Pete didn't so much manage his legions of docile charity workers as patrol the halls, like a guard at Sing Sing. His face was usually expressionless, his voice low and menacing. His timid staff cowered when he prowled. They avoided meeting with him alone, even to ask for raises. This was just how Pete liked it. I found myself looking uneasily at the air vent, right above my phone. Before I chatted with staff, I usually made sure Pete and his equally intimidating number two, Connie Favre, were out of the building, but I hadn't this time.

Sure enough, no sooner had I answered Lucette, when I was buzzed into my boss' office. I jumped and Lucette skittered back to her cubicle. As I entered Pete's corner office with windows overlooking the park, Pete waved me to a chair. I knew instantly it was bad news, since his face was brick red, which happened only when Peter Pignatelli was beside himself. Over the speakerphone I could hear the news coming straight from the whore's, I mean horse's mouth.

Freshly minted widow Hope Louis was casually dropping the bombshell that the promised $10 million was kaput. And for once I was the fly on the wall. My boss shreds most of his paperwork, answers his own phone and often leaves his secretary in the dark about his schedule. His computer screen saver warns "Don't even think about it!" Although today I could see Pete had installed a custom desk with a sunken well hiding his computer under a dark glass plate. Talk about overkill. For someone whose job it was to save the needy, Pete seemed to have a lot to hide.

At night, the janitors used Pete's office to cruise Internet porn sites. I'm sure they appreciated the privacy.

Peter turned a darker shade of mottled red as Hope Louis' voice oozed honey. She said as if bestowing a huge favor, "Pete, it wouldn't be like me to leave you high and dry. I would be happy to fund a pet therapy program."

Compared to $10 million, it was a sop. But Pete, a master at self control, merely inquired, "You mean, counseling for people who've lost their pets?"

"No," Hope said, "I mean therapy for pets. To help them express their hidden feelings. Increase their self esteem. To fulfill their deepest needs."

Pete was speechless. I almost fell off my chair.

Hope took his stunned silence as acquiescence. "You are the perfect man to find out what our little friends need, and these adorable creatures, put here on earth to serve us so loyally, deserve nothing less."

Even though, or maybe because, Hope was an insulting, double crossing wench, Pete couldn't afford to piss her off. The wealthier the caller, the quicker they would go straight to his boss to complain. Instead he genuflected.

"What an interesting idea," Pete managed.

"How does $5,000 sound?" she purred. I could just picture her using her claws to pick bits of gristle and blood from her newly veneered fangs.

"I think we can manage on that."

Of course, the therapist who did the actual work would see a few hundred dollars over several months, if that, and the rest of Hope's money would quickly evaporate into our overhead—which I soon learned upon working here, meant would find its way into Pete's pocket. That and his secret girlfriend's.

We staffers spent way too many lunches speculating about if Pete and his playmate "did it." Connie was heavy, torpid and sullen; Pete was grumpy, bald as a cue ball with liver splotches on his scalp and mean squinty eyes. The staff knew the Palm Beach Crisis Center would never attract big time donors because while the rich may run their family businesses on nepotism, they refused to give to a charity that did the same.

Sure enough, Connie Favre, her Pignatelli radar on full alert, lumbered into her lover's lair. Connie was obese with a smooth dyed platinum bob over a plump face with deep set, hooded pale gray eyes. She wore her usual camel color, the same shade as her elegant hair. Her best features were her lavishly bejeweled, professionally manicured hands and her soft, cultured voice with bewitching French accent. She was born to Algerian immigrants, of French colonial descent. Connie told us she came from a wealthy family in Paris, but once she slipped and said in the U.S., her parents worked in a bakery. One they didn't own.

Connie had been watching Pete's back since he hired her decades ago, right out of high school, to process Medicaid papers at Goodwill Industries in Reno. Pete, who was 25 years older than Connie, had been married all that time. He was married to someone else, of course. He had told her he was staying for the sake of his children, the last one having graduated college 10 years ago.

Connie tamped down her frustrating Other Woman status by sneaking Godiva chocolates from a box hidden in her desk. Then she reprimanded staff for giving clients too much food from our pantry. Every month we threw out dozens of pounds of expired canned goods.

Pete paid his political commissar 100 grand a year, plus exotic travel and bonuses, to inform on staff and concoct bizarre loyalty tests. Together they fired PBCC marriage counselors whom they suspected knew about their affair, by documenting each other's phony accusations of theft, insubordination, lying, sexual harassment, web surfing, whatever. Staff looked the other way, or got the ax.

Connie stared balefully from Pete's doorway as Hope extracted a promise that he deliver a beautiful eulogy for her newly dead husband the following day and then hung up on him. Pete betrayed his anguish with a single glance at Connie, who leaned heavily against the doorframe and settled into her usual dour, watchful state. Connie said piously, "The Louis funds would have built a safe haven in the countryside for dozens of unfortunates afflicted with mental and physical disabilities."

"Well, thanks to Hope, we'll have some pretty well adjusted cocker spaniels," I said. Connie winced, repelled by my poor taste. Pete almost smiled. Connie coughed discreetly; maybe a fudge-covered cashew had lodged in her chubby throat, around which she appeared to be wearing real pearls? Nope, clearing her throat was the signal I should get lost.

"Justine, please write a speech memorializing Vincent Louis," my boss said, his usual deadpan face and soft voice restored. "I need it by the end of the day."

"Sure thing, Pete."

Instead of going back to my office, I headed into the parking lot for fresh air. When I first got into this racket, many a fundraising pro had warned me, "It's not the work that will kill you; it's the politics." They were so right. All the hypocrisy and subservience took the stuffing right out of me.

Trust Palm Beach to put the vile, in servile.

Chapter 7

THE GETAWAY OF "SILVER FOX"

*A*fter dealing with Hope over the phone and my boss and his consort in the flesh, I needed to feel human again. But a delousing in Clorox was impractical. I grabbed the cell phone out of my purse as I headed to my car.

"Society."

"Donna? Did you see the *Post* this morning?"

"What about it?"

"There was bupkes on the Louis murder."

"You should see what I've got for tomorrow," Donna bragged. Then she made me beg.

"What?"

Donna paused. "What have YOU come up with, Justine?" she asked significantly, reminding me I wasn't keeping up my end of our private investigation into the Island murder.

"More bupkes," I admitted.

"Well, let me show you how it's done," Donna said. "Guess who was the last to see Louis alive?"

Oooh, I hadn't thought of that. A critical lead. "Who?"

"Lee Jiminez."

"Lee?" I knew Lee through business. She sold ads for the *Palm Beach Post*. Even though I explained our agency had no ad budget, she still tried to sell me space. Recently I took her up on an introductory offer for some free classifieds to sell some donated cars, when I knew darn well I wasn't going to buy any ads. I still felt guilty.

"And that's not all," Donna said. "The cops also questioned the Guatemalan landscapers. They got sick to their stomachs."

"Why?"

"They saw the rathole where the landscapers live."

Desperate illegal immigrants tend America's finest estates while subsisting in Third World squalor in nearby West Palm Beach. Five serfs pay $550 a month to share rooms with chicken-wire covering broken windows, raw sewage, monster bugs and rats the size of cats.

"The cops told me a groundskeeper showed them a hole in the ceiling where rain pours on his bare, stained mattress," Donna said. "The roof looked like it was about to cave in."

"Sounds like a motive to me." Palm Beach was long overdue for some rage against the rich.

"Not really. The men said it was easier for them to work than to rest at home. So we can eliminate them as homicide suspects."

Donna knew the slumlord from the charity circuit. "He's a major donor to the American Heart Association."

"He can afford to be," I said.

"Mr. Heartless has made almost $1 million on those tenants since he was first cited about 10 years ago. At the last Heart Ball his wife chaired, he told me he's being unfairly singled out and can't afford to pay for repairs."

Gag. "What about the owners of these landscaping companies?" I asked.

"They claimed they didn't know anything. They hire day laborers off the books. No taxes, no records."

"OK, so we're back to Lee Jiminez. What was she doing with the likes of VIP Vince?" I asked.

"Dropping off an ad proof. Hope's friends had chipped in for a full-page $5,000 tribute to the Louises, with flattering photos and adoring text, which would have run Sunday. It was timed for the award you guys were to have given him."

"That's some gesture," I said ungraciously. "Why can't these people ever donate to us directly?" Five thousand would be a down payment for the new accounting software we needed. At the Palm Beach Crisis Center, we still kept many records by hand, sloppily tracking payments and expenses. Pete wouldn't lay out the dough for new accounting software. He preferred the agency pay a shell company he secretly owned for a spreadsheet program he cobbled together which had never worked. We stayed out of hot water by having a board member who had been an accountant; "audit" what passed for our books. Donna didn't know. I found out by accident.

"The ladies would rather be seen in the *Shiny Sheet* then keep you guys in pencils and rubber bands," Donna explained.

True. "Speaking of socialites, how's Brenda Ecklund taking the scandal?"

"She's in deep sequestration, except for sending Trisha Goulden out to get all those party deposits back. Flowers, music, caterer, yadda, yadda."

"Donna, were you able to find out anything else?" I asked.

"Lee Jiminez is it. It's up to you to find out the rest."

Right away, I knew what she meant. Because the same company owns the *Post* and the *Shiny Sheet*, the papers are bitter rivals. Donna wouldn't set foot into her competitor's lobby, much less inveigle a staffer for tidbits of info, who would then leak her request to a *Post* reporter and scoop Donna on her own turf.

Well, I was looking for an excuse not to clean my desk. And I was already in my car. I opened the sunroof and popped in the Cyndi Lauper Greatest Hits CD.

"I'm there."

I hoped Lee wouldn't be irritated that I was picking her brains but not buying ads. On the way, I stopped at Krispy Kreme and picked up some cream filled, glazed.

Lee was friendly enough when I came in. Especially when she scented my gift. The sales rep was in her late fifties with short, choppy hair dyed several shades of red and wore a purple flowered blouse. Very down to earth kind of dame. You could tell she worked at the *Post* and not the *Shiny Sheet*.

"So I guess this means you are NOT buying any ads today?" Lee said, helping herself to the cloying, calorific treats. She didn't seem too offended by what a cheapskate I was.

"No."

I still felt ashamed, but sugar is its own consolation. I walked down to the end of the counter where it was private.

"Lee, I need to talk to you."

"'Bout what?" she said, through a mouthful of chocolate glaze.

"I hear you and I now have something in common."

"What's that?"

"Am I off the record with you?"

"'Off the record?' What is this, Watergate? I'm not a reporter—I sell ads for Pete's sake."

"Am I?"

"Yeah, sure, why not?"

"You and I were both in the vicinity when Vincent Louis," I paused and lowered my voice, "drowned." I didn't want to say the word, "murdered." I thought it would spook Lee.

"You were there, too?" she asked.

"Yeah. I don't want anyone to know about it."

"Did the cops speak with you, too?"

So the police had questioned her. I knew it. For a second I was a little miffed. What was I? Chopped liver? What hadn't they stopped by to see me?

"I'll be seeing them later today," I lied.

Lee nodded, glumly.

"I heard you were the last to see, uh, the victim alive."

She looked down. Probably two depressing interrogations in one day was two too many. I should look like I was commiserating. "Lee, you were in the wrong place at the wrong time. I mean, it's your job to show people proofs before the ads run."

"Tell me about it. Why can't these people in Palm Beach fax or buy stamps like everyone else? You think I enjoy going there in person? Like I have nothing else to do?"

"I know the feeling. Around the time you gave the proof to Mr. Louis, I was next door at the Ecklunds showing Mrs. Ecklund her publicity photos." I would never refer to that gold digger as "Brenda" to a third party. Accurate, but disrespectful.

"Oh, she is so sweet. My daughter knew her in high school. This is such a terrible thing to have to happen to her."

"So do you know if Mrs. Louis was with Mr. Louis?" I would never refer to that evil witch as "Hope" to a third party. Accurate, but disrespectful.

"I don't know where Hope Louis was. I didn't even go inside. Vince Louis met me in the driveway."

"Was he in a hurry?"

"No, not that I noticed," Lee said. "You know what, Justine?"

"What?"

"I really resented having to deliver the proof to Vincent Louis in person. But once I got there, I felt cheated. He didn't even invite me in!" She glared. "I know I shouldn't speak ill of the dead, but as long as I've dropped everything and come all that way, I want to see the house. How often do I get the chance? It was on Lifestyles of the Rich & Famous. I'll never get to see it now."

"I know what you mean," I said. "The only thing more irritating than making house calls on the Island is not getting invited inside the house. Or not even past the foyer."

And these same people who were featured in shelter magazines for their "gracious living" never bothered to offer drinks. This is south

Florida. Ninety plus degrees and humid and not even an ice cube.

I've brought canned tuna and powdered soup to some of our wretched clients in Century Village in West Palm Beach and Riviera Beach. (Despite that fancy name, the place was mostly a dump.) Even though they had to scrape meals together, they always invited me to eat. Sure, usually it was rock hard cookies with severe freezer burn, but our poorest clients welcomed their guests. Meanwhile, your average Island glamazon can't be bothered to offer a glass of tap water from her solid gold faucets.

Lee asked, "So the same thing happens to you?"

"All the time. It was months before I was granted admittance into the Ecklunds' palatial estate." I better tone it down. Lee had said she liked Brenda. As an unaffected teen, maybe.

"Really?"

"Yeah, you ever been there?"

"No."

"You heard it here first. One of Mrs. Ecklund's dressing rooms is 2,000 square feet . . . "

Lee grinned.

"And done up in orange. The whole enchilada."

"Orange? Really?" She was delighted.

"Yes, it was like being in Cinderella's pumpkin coach," I said. Maybe that's why Princess Brenda chose that color. I added, "So did Mr. Louis like your ad?"

"Basically, but he thought his picture should be bigger."

"What a surprise."

"I guess I was sore he didn't let me inside, so I kind of kidded him and said with all the honors he was getting lately, his head may start to swell."

We paused. I was thinking of his bloody skull sudsing up the chlorine.

"I didn't mean it, like it sounds," Lee said.

"Of course not. How'd he take it?"

"He was OK. He can take a little kidding."

As long as his wife is not around, I thought. "Did you tell the police you said that?"

"No. I didn't mean anything by it. It wasn't like I was threatening him, or anything. I just thought he was . . . "

"Inhospitable."

"Yeah, inhospitable."

I was a pretty good reporter but a rotten cop. I shouldn't be putting words in her mouth; I would have to watch it and not be so enthusiastic. I know what happened to Louis was a tragedy, yet this whole murder thing was way too exciting.

Lee continued, "Plus now I hear he was in the Mafia, so do you think I want it to get around that I insulted him in his last few minutes on earth?" She looked suspiciously around the lobby, where a Cub Scout troop was being led in for a tour. "I don't think so."

"I don't blame you. So I assume Louis wouldn't sign the ad proof?" There I did it again! Leading the witness. I've got to hold back.

"No, he went ahead and signed when I said that if he didn't the ad might not run on Sunday. He wasn't happy about it, but he cooperated. And then I left."

Hmmmm. What would the cops ask next? "Did you see anyone else around?"

"Yes."

"You did?" And now she brings it up? "Who?"

"A Rolls-Royce started to pull in, when I pulled out. Then he backed up. I didn't think anything of it. Mr. Louis had already gone back in. What's the big deal? Rollses are common as dirt on the Island. You know that."

"Did you tell the cops?"

"No." At this, she looked a little uncomfortable. More Mafia misgivings? Omerta Lee was really going in for the code of silence.

"What model?"

"Distinguished, very distinguished." She smiled.

"What was so distinguished, Lee?"

"The car was a real beauty, a silver, older model Corniche."

Wow, those sold for $360,000 brand new. Until the newer Phantom, the Corniche had been the most expensive model of Rolls. How many of them could there be?

"Who was driving?"

"I don't know, but he wasn't bad either, kind of the silver fox type that you see hanging around Ta-boo."

Ta-boo was a Worth Avenue watering hole where you went to see and be seen. There was nothing taboo about it really. It was just the same old obvious cruising for cash and patrons with "For Sale" stenciled on their foreheads. It was repeated hundreds of times a day in every bar, tavern and pick up joint on the Island.

It sounded like the police hadn't gotten too far. Lee couldn't be a suspect. And the cops didn't know about Silver Fox in the silver Rolls. Not that he could be a suspect. Not too many vicious murders tool around the Island in Rolls-Royces. Lamborghinis maybe. Not Rolls. However, it would still be good to know what business Silver Fox had with Louis, especially since it was late on a Friday afternoon. Why had he pulled out when he spotted Lee? Could he have known her?

"You didn't recognize the car or the driver?"

"Nope. Besides it happened so fast, and I needed to get the proof to production."

I must have looked at her a little funny.

"Justine, stop obsessing on the Rolls. Anyone who assumes whoever killed Louis drove off down Ocean Avenue is wrong," Lee said.

"They are?"

"Of course. Whoever did it must have come on foot and they probably got away by heading south down the beach."

I hadn't thought of that. Lee was shrewder than I thought, considering how easily I fooled her on the free auto classifieds. "Why do you say that?"

"Because no one would expect him to escape down the beach. The killer would have washed the blood off his hands in the surf and his tracks would disappear in the waves. Mr. Louis was murdered next door at the Ecklunds. But no one even knew he was there, so no one would be looking for him. The killer could practically stroll out of there and who would notice?"

"You have a point, Lee, you little forensic investigator, you."

"Let's just say I read a lot of murder mysteries," she said.

I considered Lee's theory. If the murderer had chosen Ocean Avenue, he likely would have been stuck in a traffic jam. Ocean Avenue was only two lanes and the part near the Ecklunds was under construction. When I had left Brenda's tangerine grotto, the street was narrowed to one southbound lane, as cops directed traffic around the backhoes. In a few minutes it would be northbound only and traffic would back up the other way.

The murderer must have known about the roadblock and so trotted over a mile down the beach where he could then enter the pool area at a resort, wash off, calmly sashay through the lobby, go to where he had parked his car and escape.

It made sense. When you come off the beach, you're sweaty and messy. The hotel pools were the only unguarded beach access points left on the Island. Even mere mortals could visit Palm Beach's resorts.

Lee had to be right. Who, among the Rum Runner swilling crowd at the sun-splashed resort, would know that our fun loving tourist was really a stealth assassin fresh from a death struggle? Maybe he wore a loud red hibiscus Hawaiian shirt to camouflage any blood spatters. On his way through the say, Four Seasons, he could stop at the bar for a celebratory $12 frozen Mudslide. Take in the scenery. Eye babes in thongs. Maybe even get some clam dip. Nothing burned calories like killing someone. Plus trodding through all that mucky sand.

I told Lee, "That would mean the murderer would have to be young, or at least physically fit."

"Yeah, it's hard to walk in the sand. Especially if he kept a steady pace over a mile."

But our physically fit killer could easily cover it in 45 minutes or so. This would mean the whole thing was planned. But if so, why, and who?

But still the Rolls beckoned me. "And the guy you saw in the Rolls had gray hair?"

"Yeah, it was thick, white and wavy. He was probably around 70 or so. That car was not stolen; he definitely belonged in it," Lee said.

"I know this is asking for too much, but did you see the license tag?" I asked.

"Yes, I did."

Now she tells me?

Chapter 8

PALM BEACH LIQUIDATION

"*Is* there anything else you forgot to mention?" I asked.

"Don't get excited Justine." Lee smacked her lips as she finished off the last piece of doughnut.

"You saw the car's tag?" I gasped.

"Yep," she paused and rummaged through crumbs in the Krispy Kreme box, "It was a Florida plate."

"Could you tell which county?"

"No," she admitted. "And as for the number, save your breath. I didn't get that either."

"That would have been too good to be true," I said. But maybe it didn't matter. A silver-haired gentlemen cruising in his Rolls could not be the same man as a crude Hawaiian-shirted raptor, running down the beach to the Four Seasons in time for the sunset luau. If Hawaiian Killer Boy even existed. None of it fit together.

I thanked Lee and promised more doughnuts for her trouble.

"Justine, the last thing I need is more food. Just do me one favor," she said.

"What's that?"

"Please don't ask me about Vincent Louis again. I want to put his death behind me."

I nodded. That was the difference between me and Lee. She was pulling away, while I was getting sucked in deeper by the minute. More and more the Louis investigation was reminding me of when I was a reporter. A real reporter, not a shabby, schleppy *Shiny Sheet* shill.

Once I sink my teeth into a really good story, I can't stop. I don't want to stop. I was pulled by this detective stuff, the stuff I don't do anymore now that I beg for the Palm Beach Crisis Center. I was sliding into Obsession and I don't mean the cheesy perfume. As soon as I reached my car outside the *Post* building, I grabbed my cell. First I did a little fact checking with an Island source. Then I called The Source.

"Society."

"Well, Donna, the police are wrong." I had a thing or two to show her.

"Yeah?"

"They think Lee Jiminez was the last to see Louis alive, but she wasn't."

Donna had been pecking her keyboard as I spoke. She wasn't typing anymore.

"She wasn't? Then who was?"

"I don't know yet, but just as Lee was leaving . . . " I then told Donna about Silver Fox in the silver Rolls.

Donna didn't say anything, but she started typing again. Fast.

"License plate?"

"In state. But Lee didn't see the number."

"OK. How did Louis act when he saw her?"

"Fine—he wanted a bigger photo of himself . . . "

"Don't they all?"

" . . . but he signed the proof and that was that." I also filled her in on Lee's Hawaiian Killer Boy theory.

"Makes sense," Donna said. "Except for his choice of wardrobe."

"One thing I do know for sure. The murderer did not escape through The Breakers."

"Oh yeah . . . " Donna said.

We both knew The Breakers had the snootiest security staff of all the Island resorts, insisting you show a guest pass before being allowed into the pool area. That included friends visiting hotel guests and well dressed society matrons paying small fortunes to attend charity lunches that brought The Breakers quite a tidy income. It was annoying. I had already phoned my parking valet pal at the hotel (who lived on tips and paid the hotel to clean his uniform). He assured me nothing unusual happened at the pool the day Louis was killed.

I concluded, "So that could mean the killer knows Palm Beach, since he knew enough to avoid The Breakers."

"Could be," Donna said.

Then she asked, "Do the police know about Silver Fox?"

"No."

"Excellent!" Donna meant that showing up the cops would make her scoop that much bigger. "This will definitely be on the front page tomorrow. My publisher is salivating." She added, "I'm sorry, Justine, but after you speak with the police, you'll be mentioned too."

I knew it, but there was nothing I could do. At least my photo wouldn't run; I was not an Island resident. "What are you going to say?"

"Just that you were at the Ecklund home somewhere around the time of death and like Brenda, you didn't see or hear a thing. Also that the police have questioned the Ecklund servants . . . ."

"All 400 of them?"

" . . . including Trish Goulden. The story will also note that the cops spoke to Lee Jiminez . . . "

"Must you mention Lee?" I asked, knowing the answer.

"Of course," Donna said, who is always thorough. "That's public record. Lee won't think you burned her. Since she doesn't live on the Island, it's not like she's big news. But there's something else that really bothers me," Donna added.

"What's that?"

"I've learned that when the police questioned Brenda Ecklund this morning . . . "

Man, I really was chopped liver! I bet they interviewed all the Guatemalan groundskeepers too. When was it going to be my turn?

" . . . she said something odd."

"Like what?" I asked.

"Brenda said she couldn't understand why Louis was inspecting the party preparations around the pool and deck area that afternoon when he had already been there that morning."

"He had? Why visit twice?" I asked.

"I don't know. Weird, isn't it?" Donna said. "I never thought of him as compulsive."

"Is Brenda sure about this?"

"No mistake. Brenda accompanied Louis on the Friday morning walk through," Donna said. "He seemed put out, but she had no idea why he'd be angry with her, since she was hosting his coronation."

"Maybe he wasn't angry with her. Maybe he was mad at somebody else," I mused. "Wow, that is strange."

Donna said, "We both know Louis' rep—he wasn't afraid to pick a fight. The guy publishes tabloids. But he never fouled his own nest. He wouldn't start feuding unnecessarily with a socialite and certainly not a neighbor. When you were with Brenda, did she say anything about Louis' morning inspection tour to you?"

"No."

"Anything at all about him?"

"No. We talked trendy tiaras until Trisha burst in."

The deeper we probed, the more confusing it got. We renewed our pact to inform each other immediately at the first new tidbit we heard.

Back at the office I learned that I wasn't chopped liver after all. It turned out I am caviar, sort of. While I had been at the *Post* talking with Lee, and then in my car talking to Donna, a Palm Beach Police Department detective had stopped by the Palm Beach Crisis Center and lay in wait for me, lurking in the lobby. But now that my time with the rubber hose had come, I felt a little hinky. On a murder case, I'd rather observe from the shadows where it's safe.

The plainclothes detective flashed his badge. I'd always wanted to see one of those.

"Justine Romanoff? I'm Sgt. Hajost of the Palm Beach Police Department. I'm investigating the murder of Mr. Vincent Paul Louis. Would it be all right if I ask you a few questions?"

He was average height, brown crew cut, hazel eyes, mid-30's. He didn't look too intimidating. I'm glad he hadn't come for me at night at home though. Having a strange man at the door would have been too creepy after what had already happened.

The receptionist, who always knew everything about everyone, drooled with curiosity. Couldn't she answer the phones? The therapists who walked past us kept their habitual neutral expressions. But when I saw the look on my boss' face, I quickly suggested to Sgt. Hajost that we take it outside. I could have asked him to my pit of an office, but I was afraid that even being the veteran of countless crime scenes, he might be repelled by the very sight. Plus, at the Palm Beach Crisis Center, the walls have ears.

I couldn't blame Pete for not wanting a police interrogation in the lobby, which might scare off clients, never mind skittish donors. We didn't need any unwanted notice. However tenuous my connection to the Palm Beach Predator was, there could be a scandal. I knew this was going to hurt me at the office later. We non-profit agencies, even in the sub-tropics, are supposed to purer than the driven snow.

I suggested we walk across the street to McDougal's. Typical sports bar atmosphere, waitresses slower than glaciers but expecting big tips because they're wearing push up bras and their pierced and tattooed bellies are hanging out. Greasiest burgers on the planet, but the chicken wings weren't bad. Sleuthing made me hungry. Or was it nerves? But did I really want to be licking my fingers in front of Palm Beach's finest? I could order a beer instead. But how could I drink liquor before the police? I couldn't decide. I was in a dither.

"You're aware of the Vincent Paul Louis murder?" Sgt. Hajost inquired as we slid into the wooden booth.

"Yes. I saw it in the paper today."

Now I know why conniving Connie was always cagey and guarded. Watching every word. Today I would be caffeine-alert. I ordered a Dr Pepper.

The detective watched me.

"You were at Mrs. Brenda Ecklund's mansion late Friday?"

"Yes."

Oh, I saw what he was getting at. I first heard about the murder from the hysterical Trisha Goulden. Yet I just said I learned about it from the newspaper. Already I had screwed up and I wasn't even guilty. Why was I so jumpy? He studied me as if I had bronze paint on my fingers from hurling that deadly, yet retrograde, garden gnome at the tabloid publisher's head. As if I would do such a thing just because his wife Hope was a rotten interview.

"Do you remember what time you came to Mrs. Ecklund's home?"

"Oh, around 3:30 or so."

"Did you happen to notice when Ms. Goulden came in?"

Trisha, what did he want with her? "No, I didn't know if she was there when I arrived. I saw her about an hour into my meeting with Mrs. Ecklund, when she told us Mr. Louis' body had been discovered in the swimming pool."

Why wasn't my drink here yet? Where was his coffee?

"Is Trisha a suspect?" I asked. She was all of five feet tall and completely compliant in her role of serving the irritating wealthy. Trisha was even less likely than me to kill someone.

Women like Trisha lived on the fringes of Palm Beach. They came from nice, connected families and once had well-to-do husbands who dumped them and the kids. The Trishas couldn't bring themselves to leave the Island where their connections meant something. The Trishas ended up as social secretaries or selling clothes from The Carlisle Collection in the living rooms of their former Junior League peers. Or they became decorators, calling themselves "interior designers." They did not become heinous, violent murderers.

"We just have to check out every lead, Miss Romanoff." Already Sgt. Hajost was irritated. I had that effect on people in authority positions.

"I'm sorry. I'm just a little surprised by this line of questioning," I said. He looked annoyed. I was digging myself in even deeper.

"I see," he said slowly. "Do you know Ms. Goulden well?"

"Not really."

"Did she ever happen to mention anything to you about Mr. Louis?"

"No." As long as I stuck to one word answers, I was OK.

"You spoke with Mr. Louis a couple weeks before his death?"

"Yes."

Wait a minute, how did the police know that? Had what I said about Hope gotten around? I had been incensed over the $65,000 remark and a tad indiscrete, maybe a bit imprudent . . . OK, I was downright nasty, in reviling her. But only to a select few. But nothing is secret on the Island for long and word had gotten out as it always does in Palm Beach.

The detective stared at me all grim eyed as I stalled.

Was I a suspect?

I signaled the waitress. She strolled over with a bored look and protruding belly over too tight shorts. Before I could beg for something to drink, Detective Hajost said, "You're not going to be here much longer."

I wasn't? Why not? Because he was going to cart me off to the county jail? It was an ugly high rise with slitted windows next to the Trump International Golf Course. I had always wanted to go to Mar-a-Lago, Trump's beach club on the Island. Instead, I would be a guest overlooking his other property.

"Was Mrs. Louis there?"

Where? Jail or Mar-a-Lago? "Yes, she was at home when I interviewed her husband."

"Did the Louises seem upset about anything?"

"No."

"Did he get any unusual phone calls or visits while you were there?"

"I was there only an hour or so. No."

The cop gave up. "If you remember anything, give me a call," he said, handing me his card. He hadn't even bothered to take notes. I gave the tarty waitress a dirty look on my way out, not that she noticed.

Chapter 9

MY SPIES ARE EVERYWHERE

I was brushing Dorito crumbs off my desk when my favorite graphics artist phoned. Rosie Sherman had designed and printed most of the Crisis Center's brochures, fund raising letters and gala invitations. She also took care of both her elderly parents.

Rosie said, "I hear you're out $10 million."

"You know about that already? I'm amazed."

"I wasn't surprised."

"Why not?"

"The Louises have stiffed a lot of people around town, including me."

"I didn't know that."

Time to get the dope on Hope. My best sources in the Louis case would be the Island's servant class who cater to the elite. They are silent, invisible, obedient and unnoticed. They see all. I got my best information about what was really going on at PBCC from people who didn't even work here.

"Remember how Hope won't let anyone call her husband Vinny?" Rosie asked.

"Yeah, too Bronxoid."

"'Vincent' sounds more legit," Rosie said.

"Like a little formality is going to fool anyone."

"Well, when Pete Pignatelli told the Palm Beach Crisis Center board about the Louis gift—he accidentally said, 'Vinny,'" Rosie said.

"Pete is terrible with names. We're lucky he didn't say, 'Ninny.'"

Rose continued, "Hope warned Pete he was on thin ice with the promised $10 million."

"For messing up her husband's name?" I asked. I had wanted to be sure this was really as petty as it sounded.

"Yes."

"Donors have reneged for far less," I agreed.

Rosie said Pete worked the faux pas to his advantage, since he blamed a staffer he had wanted to fire anyway. "Later on, Vincent chewed out Pete."

What did this gruesome twosome do, take turns? "Why?"

"Louis and his cronies all got mailed five of the same Crisis Center gala invitation."

"Oh no. They each got five of the same one?" I asked. Nothing pissed off donors more than getting redundant fund raising appeals.

"They told Vinny that the Crisis Center was wasting money and said he better force you guys to get your act together."

"The honeymoon is over," I said. "What else has Hope been up to, besides tormenting Pete?"

"At a recent ASPCA fund raiser, Lady Hope bought some pedigreed dog for $3,500."

I suggested, "Let's call him 'Mutt.'"

"Mutt died six days after Hope brought him home."

"Hope didn't hurt him, did she?"

"Justine! The one thing we can't accuse Hope of is harming an animal. She loves her pets."

"OK, it was worth a try."

"Hope was incensed and accused the ASPCA of deliberately selling her a lemon."

"A lemon?" I laughed.

Rosie continued, "Hope said the staff knew Mutt was terminally ill and then she threatened to sue if she didn't get her money back."

I asked, "Wasn't the whole point of buying that worthless Mutt to give to charity?"

"Theoretically," Rosie said. "But Hope said it wasn't the money, but the principle."

"So the principle is not to help poor defenseless pups?"

Rosie said, "Of course not. It's that no one pushes Hope around. By the time she was done, the ASPCA fired its chief operating officer and an elderly volunteer who had fed and walked the dogs for 15 years."

Maybe it would have been worse if the dog lived. What would Hope have done if the Pomeranian pooped on one of her prestigious Persian rugs?

No one knows the rich like those who work for them. I had to find out more about this tattered, tacky tabloid family. My old reporting skills kicked in. My office work could wait. I worked the phones like a bookie on steroids.

Hope Louis had been a bad girl, Genevieve Broussard, party planner extraordinaire, informed me. Genevieve was a single mom from Quebec who was putting her daughter through college.

"She'd better be a professional. I don't want her to be a glorified servant like I am," Genevieve often told me.

Today Genevieve said, "A few weeks ago Hope asked me to her home."

"Really?"

"Don't get so excited Justine. She summoned me to pick my brains about an upcoming sit down dinner under a big silk tent for 400. The theme was going to be 'Save Venice.'"

"It should have been 'Save Vincent,'" I said.

"It was going to be beautiful. Everything was going to be lit by hand dipped perfumed candles made from organic bees wax. Each table was going to have miniature leak proof golden gondolas filled with floating water lilies."

"So if a guest got drunk and knocked over a candle, the fire extinguishers would be right there. Genevieve, that is brilliant."

"I even suggested Hope hire models to dress as mermaids and lounge by the pool and waterfalls."

"Very Poseidon Adventure," I said.

"She loved my ideas. She consulted with me for over an hour," Genevieve said.

"So when's the party?"

"How should I know?"

"But aren't you the one putting it together?"

"No, Hope wanted me to do her party for free."

"What?"

"Hope said she would be doing me a big favor by allowing me to use her name as a reference."

I asked, "Did you walk out on that sea cow?"

"No," Genevieve sighed. "I can't afford to offend her, so I said I'd think about it. Hope kept my samples, including the clam shell and seed pearl mermaid bra. Do you know how much those cost?"

Hope wasn't the only one to pull that stunt. Mar-a-Lago which charges members $150,000 a year, suggests party decorators and florists work cut rate, because they should be honored to be considered good enough to work there. Tradespeople are so desperate for an "in" with the rich, they sometimes do it.

"If Island hostesses get their way, staff will pay them for the privilege of serving them," I said.

"Hope has always been cheap. I don't know why I wasted my time," Genevieve said. "Did you know that if Hope's marriage had ended in divorce, for any reason, she was limited to a $1 million pay out?"

"No! You mean Vincent forced Hope to sign a pre-nup?" I asked.

That had been rumored for years, but even Donna didn't know for sure.

"He did indeed," Genevieve said. "He even had lawyers set an annual clothing allowance. She got a raise every anniversary."

"That was no marriage," I said. "That was a business arrangement."

I asked, "Do you think Hope got rid of her hubby, because she'd get bupkes as a divorcee but would score the whole stash if she were 'widowed'?"

"No, Justine; I'm sorry to say that Hope has an alibi."

"Damn," I groaned. "How do you know?"

"I checked with one of my friends who sells dresses in a boutique on Via Mizner."

I knew the place, a chichi shop tucked in a little Roman-style alleyway off Worth Avenue, surrounded by stone fountains and bougainvillea trailing from trellises. The European ambience stimulated the shopping glands.

Genevieve continued, "While Vincent drowned in Brenda Ecklund's pool, Hope was getting fitted in her $65,000 evening gown."

I choked.

"Are you OK, Justine?"

"Yeah. It must have been a stray Dorito. Go on."

"My friend says the alterations took so long that Hope wasn't even home when the police got to her place."

"Too bad. I'd love to see the snooty wench manacled and dragged off in chains." Impartiality is so overrated.

Genevieve's revelations made me crave chocolate. Instead of shoving another 60 cents in the vending machine, I would go to one of the best places in town to satisfy my sweet tooth: the dark and deeply air conditioned lair of society photographer Andy Paulsen. Andy was my ultimate source and my favorite party photographer. Not only did Andy attend every Island do, but he also grew up in West Palm Beach. His tentacles reached from high school to high society.

As usual, Andy's studio fridge was stocked with 14 kinds of drinks, some of them non-alcoholic. On my way in, one of Andy's clients was leaving. She looked like an ex-Hooter's waitress with a few additional years; she had a good figure, tanned legs, streaked hair and lined face.

Andy passed me a bowl of salted almonds and miniature dark chocolate candy bars. "Who's the babe?" I asked, as if it were any of my business.

"I was doing a set of boudoir shots," Andy said. "It's very tedious work."

"Poor baby," I sympathized.

"I'm serious here. I would enjoy looking at the nude women, but all they do is criticize themselves. They keep whining, 'My thighs are too fat.' It takes all the fun out of it. Give it a rest already."

Hmmm, this 'soma dystopia' neurosis sounded like something the Crisis Center therapists would analyze, right before complaining about their diets.

"Is she a model wannabe?"

"No. Today's portfolio is for a guy she met in the bar of the Chesterfield last weekend. She wants him to go out with her. This way he gets to view the goods first."

At my look he said, "Her words, not mine."

That meant Hope wasn't the only businesswoman in town.

"So, Justine, when am I going to take your boudoir photos?" Andy asked for the 18th time. "They will be elegant and professional. Nothing cheesy." He actually thought he was being subtle.

"Forget about it Andy, it will never happen," I smirked. I unwrapped another Special Dark. "Speaking of professionals, what's your experience been with that hooker Hope Louis?"

"For one thing, Queen Hope made me come through the servant's entrance," he said. "Then she nickel and dimed me."

"You too?"

"She had ordered my pictures from her "Restore Versailles" gala and insisted I deliver them to her home. When I got there she had changed her mind but said I could leave them anyway."

"She changed her mind about paying you?"

"I don't think she ever planned to pay me."

"What did you do?"

"I pretended I thought she was joking, but now I'm left with $2,300 worth of useless photos." He took a Snickers. "I could bill her, but what's the use? Hope isn't dragging her bony ass to Small Claims Court any time soon."

"You think her ass is bony?" I asked.

"Don't you?"

"I heard she keeps it taut and uplifted by running on the beach in front of her palazzo."

"I heard she gets lipo, which is what I always suggest to my clients who carry on about their fat thighs."

"You do not!" I threw a candy wrapper at him. "So Andy, why is she so cheap?"

"She's typical," then Andy repeated the classic lament, "How do you think rich people get that way?"

He answered himself, "By pinching pennies. Once at the Fitzgerald estate, when I got up from the couch, the husband hobbled across the room on his cane and checked the seat cushions for change."

"Hope isn't that compulsive yet," I said. But could her boorish behavior signal trouble? Coal miners kept canaries with them because they were the first to die from a poisonous gas that was invisible and odorless. In Palm Beach, local vendors are the first to get stiffed when the wealthy are secretly struggling with money problems.

The Island was transfixed by Abe Gosman, the ex-*Forbes 400* half billionaire, who had filed for bankruptcy, with debts of $244 million. The health care magnate has the second largest home in Palm Beach, a $55 million property on six oceanfront acres on Billionaire's Row.

But I bet the dock workers knew what was in the wind when, one year after appearing in *Forbes*, Gosman tried to sell his yacht. The marina people probably knew several years before the banks did. Three top bank execs lost their jobs after they loaned Gosman money.

When Jimmy and Roslyn Carter solicit for a $250 million

endowment for the Carter Center at Emory University, they ask for cash. The late Joan Kroc, widow of the McDonald's founder, offered $100,000 cash and $3.5 million in stock. The Carters took it, although it looks like they got snookered, since Kroc later left the Salvation Army $1 billion.

Jimmy Carter had been irate when a Saudi prince, who pledged $9 million, fell 2½ years behind. The prince told the president he had the money, but was on a different timetable.

Was Hope Louis now in trouble—or was she on a different timetable?

Chapter 10

LOCAL GIRL MAKES GOOD

"Justine, if Hope and Vincent were about to slide into Chapter 11, why would they pledge $10 million to you guys?" Andy asked.

I said, "Maybe Vincent Louis was in a hurry to get his legacy cemented before creditors pounded down his 20-foot carved antique oaken doors that Hope had taken from a French monastery."

"Vincent would have dragged out the payments over 10 years," Andy said. "Who knows what would have happened by then?"

I said, "What if Louis hadn't been able to find a buyer for the *National Intruder*?"

"Intruding minds want to know."

"His asking price was too high. I saw on Google the *Intruder* peaked in the late 70's when it sold 5 million copies a week and had a readership of 43 million. Now sales are a third that."

"And those tabloid TV clones were killing him," Andy said. "Not that I watch any of those shows."

"Me neither," I lied too. "I think it was the end for Louis when the *New York Times* ran the headline, 'Elvis' Daughter Marries Michael Jackson.'"

"I wouldn't allow that rag in my bathroom."

"The *Times*?"

That's right, I get all my information from the *Intruder*. Admit it, you read it too."

"Well, it's not like I subscribe."

"Then you know that a lot of people were highly motivated to murder Vincent Louis."

"Such as?"

Andy looked at my speculatively. His eyes suddenly narrowed and an uncharacteristic cagey expression appeared on his ruddy, good-natured face.

"I've heard for a long time that Louis has dirty photos of one of your colleagues and I don't mean that heifer Connie Favre." He laughed.

"Who?" I was baffled.

Andy hesitated.

"Come on, Andy," I said. "Don't hold out on me. There's a box of Godiva in it for you."

"A couple months before Louis died, one of his *Intruder* stooges was said to be in the market for photos of a 'young lady' partying with one of our Tallahassee boys who is now up in Washington."

"You mean there are boudoir shots being circulated that YOU didn't take?"

"There are."

"Who?" This was explosive.

"Think Justine. Someone who has a body worth looking at."

"At PBCC? You must be kidding!" I thought about everyone I worked with at "Yenta Central." Then I thought about them with their clothes off. Yech. I gave up.

"Tell me!"

"Felicia Harold."

The mind reeled. Yeah, Pete's assistant had a nice shape and legs up to here, but she was just a small-time embezzler with big-time implants.

"Why would a civilian like her interest the tabs?" I asked.

"Vincent Louis wasn't gunning for Felicia. She's the small fish who got caught in his net. Louis was after her former lover," Andy smirked.

"Which one?" I asked. "There've been so many." OK, so I was jealous. Well at least I could feel self righteous about it. It's not like I had to worry about my bare butt appearing in the tabs anytime soon. For which I'm sure everyone is grateful.

"Senator Vernon Randall," he answered.

I gasped. Sen. Randall in a scandal? With our very own Felicia? Andy laughed at the shocked look on my face.

He explained, "Louis obtained photos of Felicia undressed and getting busy with one of her married professors."

"When was this?"

"Back in her stoner college days," Andy said.

"Before Randall became the Family Values Senator," I said.

Andy quoted the Senator's famous speech, "Tabloid publishers are pornographers who degrade American family life. They are lower than the drug dealers on our cities' most crime ridden streets and even Janet Jackson."

The Senator had said Louis, Howard Stern and Bubba the Love Sponge should be fined several hundred thousand dollars apiece. "The First Amendment was never meant to protect this scum."

Andy noted, "Louis has a network of more than 10,000 informants who could find dirt on anyone. Some of them are here in town right now."

"Andy, you're not really saying Senator would hire a hit man?"

Andy grinned. "No, Justine, I'm saying that Felicia Harold has even more to lose than the Senator."

"How could that be? She's not an elected official."

"Her father will cut her off for doing drugs."

We both knew Mr. Harold chaired the local chapter of Just Say No.

"He already put Felicia on probation because she stole from the family," I said. "Ever since she's been trying to get back into his will."

"Right," Andy said. "If Daddy finds out Felicia takes after Gov. Jeb Bush's daughter, he will disinherit her."

"There are plenty of other people who hated Louis," I said.

"Did you know in his early twenties he was with the CIA?"

I hadn't known that. "You think at this late date that matters?"

"No. I think it's the Mafia."

"In Palm Beach? No way."

"Louis had a godfather who was a real life Godfather, Mob boss Frank Costello. He's the one who bankrolled Louis $25,000 to start the *Intruder*. The deal was, Louis' tabs would lay off the Mob."

"But he declared open season on everyone else," I said. Louis lead the charge against Jackie Kennedy, which must have been agonizing for Hope. I wonder if the First Lady had ever snubbed her?

"Louis' tactics are as dirty as ever. He hires people to falsely accuse actors of child abuse and get the law to investigate. Then the *Intruder* covers the monster it created. And look how he taped Frank Gifford having sex with that skanky stewardess."

"I heard Louis never got over the Carol Burnett case," I said. She was one of the few who took on the *Intruder* and won. Liz Taylor sued for $20 million and got nowhere. Johnny Carson took him on and Louis printed nastier stories about him.

"Louis attacked the celebrities who challenged him and protected the ones who informed on other celebs," Andy said.

He added, "The *Intruder* still taps phones illegally, steals mail, bribes people and hacks into celebrities' phone and credit records—even the late Frank Sinatra!"

"I thought he had promised to lay off Mob associates." Then I tried to top Andy.

"Louis offered $100,000 to a retired Colorado police detective to talk about JonBenet Ramsey. He refused. Then Louis sent the cop photos of his dead mother who had killed herself when he was six. That was how he found out how she really died."

"So the classic question is, not who would want Louis dead, but who wouldn't?"

"Exactly, but I still think it's the Mafia."

"Why?"

"I heard talk at the Rotary that the feds are looking into the Mob bribing brokers to tout worthless stocks and Louis' was getting a percentage of the profits. The Mob warned Louis not to testify or they'd cut off his balls."

I gulped as Andy chomped a Milky Way. "Holy shit! You heard all this at a Rotary meeting? This sure beats the Serenity Prayer."

I added, "Andy, if the Mob already warned Louis to keep his mouth shut, why drown him?"

"Whoever killed Louis didn't know him too well," Andy said.

"How do you know?" I still suspected that Hope had bought her alibi from the dressmaker.

"Vince couldn't swim. All the hit man . . . "

"The murderer, you mean."

"All the hired gun had to do was shove Vincent really hard into the deep end. Louis would have panicked and gone right under."

"You're kidding."

"My Rotary pals say Louis had hated the water since a childhood boating accident."

"But Louis had the pool and yacht and $11,000-a-month boat crew with white uniforms and gold braid!" I said.

"All accoutrements expected of a resident of Billionaire's Row," Andy assured me.

"So by his overkill, the killer risked being spattered with his victim's blood and leaving prints on the murder weapon," I said.

"The killer was someone who hated Louis enough to kill him, but someone who didn't know him well," Andy concluded.

"That rules out our Hope."

Rats.

Chapter 11

PUTTING THE "FUN" IN FUNERAL

Even at work, I couldn't get enough of Vincent Louis—the man, the myth, the Mafioso. I still had to draft the eulogy for my boss, so intruding minds want to know, how many different ways were there to say "blessed saint?" I was reaching for the thesaurus when Donna rang.

"Where have you been? I've been trying to reach you."

"I was investigating the Louis case."

"Did you find out anything?"

"I discovered all kinds of sordid stuff."

"Great," Donna said.

"Yeah but, the bottom line is Hope didn't do it."

"Crushing blow, Justine."

"Tell me about it."

"You sound like you need to have your spirits lifted."

"That's about the only thing I can afford to lift. Anyway, what do you have in mind?"

"Let's you and me put the 'fun' back in funeral," Donna said.

Ugh. As a Palm Beach Crisis Center vassal, I was expected to attend the Louis funeral so the agency could keep up appearances. My boss Pete attended dozens of rich men's funerals a year, even though we usually weren't in the will. Once the father-in-law of a serious donor to a related agency died and Pete hadn't heard about it. He found out when the grieving son—who had never given us a dime—gave $1 million to an animal shelter to teach us a lesson for being disrespectful to his family. Ever since, Pete checks the obits first thing in the morning.

I did not want to go to Vincent Louis' funeral, because I didn't belong in Island circles. But as long as Donna was there, I could hack it. However, I drew the line at wearing my staff photo ID to the funeral. I didn't have to be obvious about being a paid mourner.

Once we entered the Episcopal Church of Bethesda-by-the-Sea, next to The Breakers, Florida and the 21st century faded away. The imposing building was built of stone with dark alcoves, secret spaces and lots of carved wood. As we entered the anteroom before the sanctuary, we heard the low voices of mourners.

"This summer I'll be taking a luxury trip to Venice and I'll be writing it off."

"How did you swing that?"

"I'm paying to restore an old palace along the Grand Canal. I'll get to meet some viscounts."

The IRS would probably be the only grief stricken presence in this room. As soon as the ladies spotted Donna, they dropped the Eurotrash talk and rushed to greet her. Donna was kind enough to introduce me.

"Countess Elsa von Graff, this is Justine Romanoff." Countess Elsa looked way too young for such a high falutin name. She was in her early twenties, very pretty and slender with soft, light brown hair.

"I am so pleased to meet you," Elsa said. "Are you related to the

St. Petersburg Romanoffs?"

"Yeah, the St. Petersburg, Florida, Romanoffs," I said. Elsa looked puzzled for a moment, then laughed. Well, at least she had a sense of humor; not many on the Island did when it came to their supposed pedigrees. I was a Romanoff the way the late Mike Romanoff, the Beverly Hills restaurateur, was. He was born to a poverty-stricken Jewish tailor in Russia and ran away from several orphanages—all the way to Ellis Island. Once on U. S. soil he claimed to be Queen Victoria's cousin. Although ol' Vic used to say she was descended from King David.

Since I'm Jewish, I'm a closer match to King David than the Queen of England. Be that as it may, in the 1930's Mike Romanoff opened a hit restaurant in Hollywood with golden crowns painted on the doors. Maybe my grandfather thought the royal Romanoff name would bring him luck. He must have assumed no U. S. citizen would know the difference.

But this isn't America. This is Palm Beach where the gentry lives and dies by bloodlines.

Former Mayor Paul Ilyinsky was a grand-nephew of Czar Nicholas II. The late mayor had attended the funeral of the remains of his Russian relatives, whom the Bolsheviks executed in 1918. Another former Palm Beach mayor, Yvelyne "DeeDee" Marix, was said to be related to Charlemagne and her sister was a French countess.

Other Islanders stamped their platinum cards with titles such as, "Jane Smythe, Baroness of Ashford." This was to really impress the local cocktail waitress. The "baronesses" then cadged free drinks in the VIP sections at Island clubs.

Donna was chatting up the young 'countess.'

"Elsa, you should speak with Justine about your efforts to open a Palm Beach chapter of the Leukemia Association. Justine works for a local charity and has great ideas on marketing and publicity."

That was a surprise. Why would a carefree 'countess' be interested in such a tough project? There were a lot easier ways to make money and she didn't look like she needed the dough. Or maybe she needed a slush fund? Many a Palm Beach charity had served as a cover for that sort of thing.

"I'd be happy to talk with you," I said. "In the meantime Elsa, here's some free advice. If someone gives you money, give her a plaque and announce her name at a luncheon. If you don't, she'll badmouth you."

"Always observe the Palm Beach 'honor system,'" Donna said. "If you don't honor them, you're not in the system."

"Thanks. I'll remember that," said Countess Elsa.

Donna and I strolled around the dark anteroom. She whispered, "Elsa's Jewish, by the way."

That was a stunner. "What? 'Countess' von Graff? Don't tell me she's another fake 'Duchess of Umbria?'"

"It's a long, wild story, I'll tell you about it sometime," Donna said. "Elsa is here at the funeral because she wants Hope to see her and consider donating money in Vincent's memory for leukemia research."

"Why?"

"A few years ago, Elsa's life was saved by a bone marrow transplant. She moved here from Washington, D. C. for the climate."

Wow. You can't judge a book by the cover, although surviving leukemia didn't make 'Countess' Elsa von Graff a saint.

Besides, I would soon have to confront a devil who had said I wasn't worth $65,000. I could try to discreetly avoid Hope, but she was the type who, no matter what the circumstances, would do a census of every person, what they were wearing and how much they paid.

No one would screw with Donna Shaughnessy though. She would be my Rock and Protector. At least I looked like I fit in; I had just bought a very businesslike, yet chic, dark gray Yves St. Laurent cashmere suit at the church's thrift shop, The Church Mouse. Not all the Island fashionistas kicked their clothing to the curb for garbage men to scavenge. Some give their castaways to consignment shops, such as The Church Mouse, which makes $300,000 a year.

Plus I was squiring my "Burberry" purse from Target. A

handsome $18 special, I was still kicking myself that I hadn't picked it up on sale for $14 the week before. This handbag was one of the better knockoffs I ever bought.

We entered the inner sanctum, OK the lounge, where Hope held court behind Jackie O sunglasses. Her hair was done up with a little black hat and veil. She was gracefully perched in a very formfitting suit with skirt shorter than it should have been for her husband's interment. She had great legs, set off by black hose with little sparkles. She wore intense four-inch heels attached to bondage shoes with criss crossing black leather straps and metal grommets. Maybe Hope was looking to pick up a gladiator.

Without Donna, I wouldn't have had the courage to approach the throne, er couch, where Hope was surrounded by a swarm of sycophants who sympathetically squeezed her shoulders and offered the widow comfort she apparently didn't need. "She must be in shock," they murmured.

Hope ignored them all as she slowly raised her shades to appraise me and I filled with dread. Her cruel eyes were bone dry as she examined me as coldly as a mortician pulling the sheet off a corpse on the slab. The Black Widow rendered verdict:

"You're wearing my daughter's old suit."

I heard muffled gasps and laughter and my face felt scorched as everyone stared at me. I was guilty as charged. I had bought secondhand clothes. No one spoke as I stood there with a sick frozen smile and felt nauseous.

Then Donna broke the stunned silence. "You must be in shock," she said to Hope, kindly, yet, with an edge beneath her voice. "We are so sorry for your loss."

The scary, make that merry, widow barely acknowledged Donna's condolences. She slipped her shades back down her ski jump nose and offered her pale cheek for an air kiss, to a mourner who was dressed retail. Donna took my arm and guided me out of the snake pit.

"Hope must be in shock," I said as we entered the sanctuary. "Didn't she see my purse?"

"If she had, she would have said something about discount houses," Donna agreed.

"Well at least my accessories are brand new," I explained. I was joking around but I was sweating under my cashmered armpits. If Donna hadn't rescued me, a mob with pitchforks would have grabbed me, dragged me up to the bell tower by my hair and thrown me into the bonfire set up in the parking lot. I had sinned by posing as an equal. It was unforgivable that I got caught.

At least Donna would keep my sartorial comeuppance out of the *Shiny Sheet*. Being an heiress who was the Island's ultimate social arbiter, Donna could get away with her natural hair color, little make up, not being anorexic and a dowdy cotton shift sprinkled with little blue cornflowers. On her, lack of frou frou was a symbol of her independence and incorruptibility. Donna Shaughnessy was so far above everybody, she didn't have to try. The Emperor had no Designer Clothes. But at critical social occasions such as this, the society editor always wore an "important" piece of jewelry, as Sotheby's would say.

"Nice pearls, Donna," I said appreciatively.

"Nice duds," she said. I could tell she felt bad since she had never commented on my clothes before.

"You mean, I was a dud," I muttered.

"Oh, ignore her. We've got bigger fish to fry," Donna said. "We need to look for the legion of Vincent's mistresses that must be swarming all over the place."

"Tell me if you spot Felicia Harold," I said.

"She wasn't sleeping with Vincent," Donna stated. "I would have known."

"No she wasn't. I want to see if she brought her new boyfriend."

"I didn't know Felicia was dating anybody."

"With the kind of shoes she's been wearing lately, she is definitely seeing someone," I said.

My suspicion was confirmed when we spotted Felicia near the back of the sanctuary greeting her mother. Felicia displayed her bod in a black, clingy knit Chanel dress, with white blanket stitch trim, a big white gardenia on the lapel and black silk shoes trimmed in ropes of pearls. I want shoes like that! I could never walk on those awe inspiring stilettos. Felicia must have a foot fetish. Maybe she was a lapsed Catholic.

"Is that the new talent?" Donna appraised Felicia's beefy escort, who kept sneaking peeks at Felicia's feet. "I thought I knew all the town gigolos."

"He is some definite arm candy," I said.

Felicia's escort was a tall Latin lover, with dark face, thick black hair slicked back, long lashes and slightly bucked teeth. He had broad shoulders and a great body. He looked a little uncomfortable in his suit as if he'd prefer something in leather and sweat. I noticed something dark was under his nails.

Always the model of decorum, especially at a society funeral, Felicia caught my eye, then winked lasciviously. Felicia was class with a capital "K."

I didn't have a chance to go over and meet the Latin Lover because dainty Trisha Goulden had rushed over to me on her size four feet. She looked desolate, yet very well coordinated.

"Trisha. Are you OK?" I asked.

She signaled me to come closer. "The police questioned me. You?"

"Yeah, me too. It wasn't so bad." I figured this wasn't the place to tell her Detective Hajost asked about her.

"They asked about you," Trisha said. She looked at me as if I had a collection of deadly bronze botanical missiles tucked in my Burberryish bag. As we were seated, her nervousness almost made me look forward to the ceremony. I avoided looking at the open coffin. One thing about Jewish funerals, there was never an open coffin.

I was sorry not to sit next to Felicia. Not only did I want to learn more about her Latin Lover, but Felicia knew the price of everything. She often advised me, "Never fall for what you read in the fashion rags. They lie every time about haute couture prices." She had said a "very simple wool day dress" cost $15,000 while cocktail wear would set her back by $24,000 to $50,000.

Felicia had added, "Add embroidery and the sky's the limit."

Towards the end of the ceremony, my boss ascended the altar for his command performance. Arf! Arf! Or as Peter Pignatelli's secret girlfriend would say, "Appearances must be observed." I swiveled my head. Pete's wife was near the front on the right and Connie was in the last pew on the left. Her head was modestly bowed.

Pete intoned, "It was the greatest privilege of my life to have known a good hearted, generous man such as," he hesitated ever so slightly, "Vincent Paul Louis."

I had bold faced the deceased's name and put it in huge type so Pete would get it right. Hell hath no fury like a donor whose name is mispronounced. Like everything else, such insolence would be grounds for cutting us off.

"Vincent gave to worthy causes because he truly cared about the less fortunate," Pete recited with deep sincerity.

Did I mention that I really wanted a career in fiction? Thank you Palm Beach Crisis Center for making my dream come true.

"I had to convince Vincent that we wanted to change the name of the agency to his name as recognition of his generous support," Pete read. "Even that small gesture would have been inadequate for such a heroic personage."

Did I say I wanted to write fiction? Make that science fiction.

Then Pete departed from my notes and winged it like a pro. "Vincent was gracious. He fled from gratitude; he was deeply reluctant to be honored. Vincent Paul Louis hated accolades, preferring to do what was right and letting the other guy take the credit."

Wow! You could tell Pete used to be a therapist, because his poker face never betrayed him. I was watching the master in action. Truly, I was not worthy. Hope appeared regal and gratified, accustomed by divine right to lackeys (even those making $175,000 annually) carrying out her orders.

Pete stopped short of tugging his forelock, but he came through like a trooper. The word hadn't gotten out yet the $10 million was a bust and Louis looked like a hero.

Then Pete listed the various good works to which the Louises had given. "Today is a fitting occasion to honor the deceased for his many generous gifts to:"

The Vincent Paul Louis and Hope B. Louis College of Nursing at Good Samaritan Hospital, as well as The Vincent Paul Louis and Hope B. Louis Cardiac Surgery Unit at St. Mary's Hospital."

(The last two were because Louis had already had a triple bypass. Who knew his heart wasn't going to be the problem?)

Pete continued, "As a standard bearer for journalism, the deceased also contributed to The Vincent Paul Louis and Hope B. Louis Eminent Scholar Chair in Newspaper Publishing at the Vincent Paul & Hope Louis Business School at Florida Atlantic University and The Vincent Paul Louis and Hope B. Louis First Amendment Institute at the Vincent Paul & Hope B. Louis College of International Communications at Palm Beach Community College."

"This is a truncated list," Pete droned. "He also donated to the Vincent Paul Louis and Hope B. Louis Center for Caring . . . "

Center for Caring? For a guy who didn't care about credit, Louis sure had splashed his name everywhere. If these top donors were so interested in "the family legacy," how come none of them ever named anything after their parents? Soon we'd be hearing about the inevitable Hope Baylor Louis Home for Unwed Mothers at the Hope Baylor Louis Center for Teenaged Mutant Ninja Turtles, blah, blah, blah.

And what about my legacy? Well the powers that be could name the Justine Adelle Romanoff Women's Room right off the janitor's closet at Palm Beach Crisis Center. The one with the broken tampon dispenser that was never fixed because most of the people who worked there were centuries past menopause.

Frick, Morgan, Carnegie and Mellon did not put their names on every public institution they funded. Nor did a Seattle woman who recently and anonymously gave tens of millions to civic causes, as well as a duty shop king who had secretly contributed $600 million. Someone else quietly gave $360 million to Rennselaer Polytechnic

Institute.

I remembered from Sunday school, "One who gives charity in secret is greater than Moses." But anonymous giving accounts for less than 10% of the donations over $1 million. Here in Palm Beach County, museums are offering naming rights to toilet stalls.

I had thought about ending Pete's eulogy with a quote from the *Wall Street Journal* editorial. "Besides anonymity, the other idea fundamental to charity is that it should really cost you something. However wealthy you are, you are supposed to experience self-denial. Since today's named donors can clearly afford their generosity in financial terms; maybe the "cost" of their gifts should be ego gratification. Talk about giving till it hurts."

You can see why I left it out.

Pete finished with what he persuasively claimed was Vincent's lifelong motto, "Give while you live, so you know where it goes." He bowed his head modestly. No one knew yet there would never be a Hope Baylor Louis Palm Beach Crisis Center.

But I would be proud to stencil her name on the crapper.

Chapter 12

AN ISLAND FAMILY FEUD

I should really clean my desk. Too bad my day job was getting in the way of my Louis murder investigation. I crumpled an old Cheetos bag and unearthed some cracked M&Ms. Pete shouted down the hall for me. He did that when he was stressed, which was usually. After today's church performance, I put it down to artistic temperament.

"Justine, I have a decorating assignment for you," he said with a half smile.

I put on my polite but puzzled look.

"Mrs. Louis has offered us another $5,000."

"Excellent." After Pete's turn on stage, he deserved it. But who knew how much of the money would be funneled to the agency and how much would go to please his cheesy squeeze?

"Not so fast. She has asked," (emphasis on asked, meaning ordered,) "us to display her husband's effects in the lobby."

"What effects?" I was thinking tools of the trade, blackjacks, rubber hoses, cubic zirconium.

"She has some mementos from Mr. Louis for us to display but wasn't specific. A large trophy case will be delivered to us shortly, along with a box of Mr. Louis' possessions. Please see that they are arranged."

"Hmmmm. OK." Maybe I could frame the pre-nup, since unfortunately I wouldn't be able to frame Hope for her hubby's death.

Pete was gathering his gym bag for an afternoon excursion. It wasn't a fake prop for a quickie at a no-tell motel with you know who, but to really exercise. I admired his discipline. He lifted weights and did the Stairmaster four times a week. He tried to get Connie to join him, but since he controlled everything else in her life, I think being a lazy sugar bonbon was her way of passively resisting.

Hope hadn't lost any time ridding herself of reminders of Vincent. She had given us a box of trash she didn't want around the house. The widow needed to appear sentimental, so it was on our backs. I displayed old World War II pictures and VFW awards. The Vatican photo. Some cheap tin bowling trophies, before Hope made Vincent sponsor a polo team. There was an ancient photo of young Vincent on a horse, which brought to mind one of my favorite society articles, in which Shannon Donnelly of the *Shiny Sheet* described a national equestrian show.

"The 400 deep-pocketed guests celebrated with a cocktail hour and a seated dinner, all the while keeping one eye on the pricey mounts."

"They watched the horses, too."

As I sifted Hope's garbage, I realized that in insulting me, she had inadvertently told me she had a daughter. Going online, I discovered Hope's daughter by her first marriage was flogging a movie script, promoted as, "The Godfather meets Citizen Kane." The fictional plot was that someone who resembled Hope had someone just like Vincent kill her first husband. The press appeared to think Hope's daughter was a lunatic.

Just as I was basking in the glow of Hope's misfortune, Felicia

Harold strutted in. She had changed since the funeral.

"Justine, check this out," she said, twirling in my dull, gray office wearing pink and green flowered Lilly Pulitzer cropped pants and a matching fuchsia polo shirt with kelly green johnny collar. I felt a jealous twinge. As an idealistic journalism student I had once longed for a Pulitzer. Then I came to Palm Beach, got cynical and . . . let's just say I still want that Pulitzer.

Felicia shut the door. "Lose the Burberry knock off," she ordered me. As she perched on my guest chair, I admired her insouciant green wedgie sandals, with pink feathered tassels.

"What happened today at church was a crime," she declared.

"That Louis' cold blooded murder runs free?"

"No, that you appeared in public wearing an obvious counterfeit."

"What's wrong with that?" I was offended.

"There's nothing wrong with wearing designer substitutes, but make sure they are so close to the real thing that people like Hope can't spot them from a mile off in a dank church."

She added, "I'll let you in on a fashionista secret. You need to go to 'Gucci Gulch.'"

"What's that?"

"It's a little piece of heaven. It's where a woman sells hot designer goods out of her garage in Broken Sound."

Broken Sound? That was no flea market; it was a tony, gated enclave in Boca Raton, the southernmost city in Palm Beach County. The "garage" in this million-dollar home looked like a professional showroom, Felicia said, stocked with half a million in Gucci, Prada and Dior merchandise. All very hush hush and on the QT.

"Don't tell me. You heard about this from your Support Group for the Wealthy?"

Felicia smugly nodded. My entrepreneurial colleague was starting to remind me of Catch-22's Milo Minderbinder, the World War II mess officer who ran a worldwide underground trading syndicate right from his squadron. The only difference was Milo wore combat boots and Felicia preferred Jimmy Choos.

"You can't go there by yourself, Justine. It's by appointment only and you have to be accompanied by someone the Gucci Gulch gal knows."

Even the underworld is filled with snobs in Palm Beach County. It sounded like Felicia's fence could maintain the membership list at the exclusive Bath & Tennis Club on the Island. I always wondered why there are so many clubs named "Bath?" Didn't these people shower at home?

Felicia added, "You can get a leather Louis Vuitton bag for $400. The kind that's special ordered from France and takes six months to deliver. Even the tag says, 'Manufactured in France.'"

"In English?"

"In French! These are very convincing counterfeits," Felicia said. "On Worth Avenue you'd have to pay $700."

This Boca black market was Felicia's idea of a bargain?

"If you want to give your mother a gift, this woman has the counterfeit packaging too."

"I don't think so, Felicia. I would never spend $400 on a purse. And my mother would kill me if I did, not that I'd be dumb enough to tell her."

"Are you sure? We should go before she gets busted."

"Who?"

"My supplier, not your mother."

"Thanks, but no thanks. I'll stick with Tar-jay."

The always pragmatic Felicia dropped it. Time for office gossip. She apparently had no clue that Vincent Louis possessed her incriminating coed photos and I wasn't going to let on. Felicia focused on the confines of the Crisis Center.

"Well," she said with a nasty smile, "it looks like our little CPA is on the way out." Felicia swung her flowered legs over the arm of the chair, so I could see the pink embroidery on the sides of her Manolo Blahniks and her perfect, hot pink pedicure.

"What are those shoes made from, Felicia? Flamingo?"

"The only accessories I wear are made from the hide, fur or

feathers of endangered species," Felicia said with a smart ass grin. Though in her past life Felicia had been an accountant, not that she dressed like one, she was still sensitive about not being a CPA. It was just as well considering her fondness for cooking the books at the family firm. But when the Palm Beach Crisis Center for the first time in its 50 years hired a CPA to be chief financial officer—Felicia was miffed. I think she wanted to redeem herself as our first CFO because she had something to prove to her father.

Since coming to the Crisis Center Felicia had completed her 500 hours of community service and surprised us all by sticking around. She had made herself indispensable to Pete. First, she proved herself by forbidding therapists to offer Kleenex to crying clients, because tissue cost too much. Felicia was the enforcer when someone used too many paper clips or rubber bands. Pete made us pay for our own calendars and schedule books (while he and Connie got new Palm Pilots every year) but it was Felicia who now micromanaged office supplies as he would wish.

Then Felicia sent a solicitation letter to her wide circle of Island acquaintances to donate us cash and goods and brought in $30,000 in merchandise over three weeks. Pete was impressed. After that Felicia worked like a stevedore. Donors offered us their furnishings and appliances as long as the Palm Beach Crisis Center did the cleaning and schlepping.

I was shocked when I first saw a smudged Felicia in tennis shoes and dusty work clothes at the office.

"Felicia, is that you?"

"You should see the shit hole I just came from," she groaned. "Literally. I just spent four hours cleaning out an old man's apartment. He was incontinent."

I started to laugh.

"And he collected porn. Stacks and stacks of magazines and videos." She sighed.

"Did you watch them?"

"He had four VCRs. None of them worked."

But I wasn't so sure Felicia was up to the biggest part of her job, which was selling donated used cars.

"I finally persuaded my Dad to donate his $4,600 Cadillac to us, he can afford it," one of my caseworker friends had told me. "Then a couple weeks later he gets a note written by Felicia, signed by Pete, thanking him for his tax deductible gift of $2,300. Now he thinks we're all a bunch of charity case incompetents."

"But why would we sell cars for half of what they're worth?" I was baffled.

"Dad says nonprofits only hire people who can't hack it in business."

Once Felicia had cemented herself as the go to girl for all the detail work involved in collecting cars, boats, durable goods, condos and timeshares—she asked for a salary. Pete, having gotten used to her working for free, naturally didn't want to pay.

"Felicia, you don't need the money," he said, "besides no one makes any money in this shop."

"My Support Group for the Wealthy gave me the courage to do this," she intoned solemnly.

Pete cut to the chase. "If we hire you, we'll have to lay off someone else, someone who really needs the income," he said, furrowing his brow in feigned concern. However, Felicia's Palm Beach Crisis Center therapy made her impervious to his attempted guilt trip.

"If you respect me and the work I'm doing, my being independently wealthy is irrelevant."

Later when layoffs came and Pete said she had to go, Felicia begged. She flattered. She wheedled. Pete brought on Felicia and let go his secretary, who had a sick mother at home. Pete told staff Felicia was still a volunteer, although we all knew she was now similar to Connie, a paid informant. The jury was out on sex privileges. For $30,000 a year, I don't think Felicia would waste her time.

Even though Felicia had reformed, her father still seemed to despise her. Felicia not only dressed as well as Grace Kelly; she had the same type of father who treated her with contempt.

And now Felicia was griping about our newly hired CPA.

"So what's wrong with Penny?" I asked.

"She was dumb enough to tell Pete she had caught him red handed."

I raised my eyebrows and signaled her to lower her voice, even though the door was already shut. There was a lot of eavesdropping in our rabbit warren of cubicles.

"You know that Milwaukee conference Pete and Connie attended recently?"

"Yes." I whispered, "They rented separate rooms, talk about a waste of agency money."

"Afterwards, they stayed at the five diamond American Club resort in Kohler, Wisconsin, an hour north. Typical. But then someone charged $800 worth of lawn and garden equipment from a Wisconsin store on the agency credit card."

"No way," I said. Neither of them had a green thumb.

"Then the new accountant told Pete, 'I refuse to pay this.'"

"Her days are numbered," I said. "How'd the boss take it?"

"He was stunned for maybe a second and then blamed his beloved Connie. He said he had no idea Connie had gone shopping nor how she got the agency credit card and it must all be a terrible mistake."

I asked, "Can't they spend agency money here, so we don't have to pay for shipping?"

Felicia knew everything about everybody. She knew that while staff was being told we were running huge deficits, the board was told we were doing very well. She knew while we were bleeding red ink, Pete was traveling around the country presenting papers and earning double dipping consulting fees re: "Financial Management of Non-Profits." He even sold accounting software for personal profit he had designed on agency time that crashed Crisis Center computers several times a day.

Felicia said, "When our new accounts payable clerk told me she billed for $8,500 that week, Pete reprimanded her to keep all her work confidential or she would be fired."

"He says that to everyone," I reminded her.

"Did you hear Pete just chewed out several of our top geriatric social workers because they showed their time sheets to the man who is funding their program, rather than letting Connie doctor them first?"

"Yes, but Pete treats you pretty well," I observed.

"True," she said. "I don't need the money and can leave at any time."

"Felicia, why don't you tell me what's really going on?" I asked. I might as well pry into her love life, since I couldn't press her about the Louises. If my mental health colleagues heard about my morbid obsession, they were legally empowered to throw me in the rubber room.

Let's not tempt fate.

Chapter 13

DESSERT, BUT NOT JUST DESSERTS

"*W*hat do intruding minds want to know?" Felicia asked me. She coyly fluffing her flamingo feathered footwear with fingernails the same color fuchsia.

"Who's your hot new boyfriend? And how does he like your new shoes?" I knew Pete was into bondage, but of the employee, not the fetish variety. And I knew that Felicia had to have a lover, probably that man I saw at the Louis funeral, or Connie would have gotten rid of her already and made Pete think it was his idea.

I had learned more about Felicia's new boy toy since the funeral. A fellow staffer at the church recognized him as the owner of a nearby garage that inspected and valued all our donated cars. He then sold them for us with him getting a little fee. Latin Lover had once tried to sell my friend $250 in repairs she didn't need. Nice try.

It was clever of Felicia; her boyfriend saved the Crisis Center from having to pay for ads and giving people test drives. Plus he was convenient for quickies. It was a cozy arrangement, but our staff who drove disabled residents to doctors appointments got stranded because the tires Latin Lover sold us kept blowing out. Then he charged us for new tires.

Felicia smiled. "He's so studly . . . " she began.

"But he's no Joey Buttafuoco," I finished. "And I mean that in a nice way."

"Sorry, he doesn't have a twin brother," she said snidely. Ouch! Touche.

"So what's his name? Or do you guys talk?"

I once had a college room mate who sampled every foreign exchange student on campus, sort of the Grand Tour, and the less English they spoke, the better. She liked them Spanish.

"His name is Manuel," Felicia laughed. "He's from Venezuela. I call him Manny."

"'Manly Manny', I like the sound of that."

Felicia was practically licking her lips. I guess she didn't mind a little sleaze with her grease.

"Justine, are you sure you don't want to go to Gucci Gulch? It would be fun," Felicia asked.

"Nah, I don't want to waste that lady's time. I'm not going to buy anything." I still had to figure out a way to hold down my job and still get local Island gossip on the Louises. Then I had a brilliant inspiration.

"Felicia, there is one thing I'd like to do," I said. "I'd like to accompany you to the Support Group for the Wealthy and write it up for the *Shiny Sheet*. It would be a perfect publicity opportunity for Palm Beach Crisis Center."

"Do you promise not to use any names?"

"Of course not."

"What about photos?"

"I'll shoot the therapist from the front and the attendees from the back only."

Felicia knew Pete strongly encouraged staff to cooperate with me to get us in the paper. Especially the Island's favorite rag.

"Well, you're in luck, Justine. Our next meeting is the day after tomorrow at 10:00, so meet me at 1313 Mammon Lane #PH-1."

I knew "PH" meant "penthouse," but I couldn't place the address. "OK, where is that exactly?" Then Felicia gave me the biggest surprise so far that morning.

"It's in the slums of Palm Beach."

Chapter 14

BLACKMAIL ON MIDAS STREET

The latest edition of the *Shiny Sheet* was a shocker for what it didn't say. There was just a boring article listing the names of the eminences who attended the funeral of the Tabloid King, accompanied by tasteful photos of bereaved tax dodgers. The paper quoted Pete at length.

What went wrong? I sensed the long, fully depilatoried arm of Hope B. Louis.

Donna explained all at Testa's, a restaurant that had been around forever, a few doors down from her newsroom. It was weird how Florida restaurants often did not serve fresh fish, even a few blocks from the ocean. I'd wanted to meet at the Golden Calf on Midas Street, but Donna didn't eat red meat.

We ate outside so we could people watch. Holiday shoppers promenaded under 30-foot tall Royal Palm trees festooned with red velvet ribbons and twinkling Christmas lights. The first words out of my mouth, after ordering the strawberry pie as my entrée were, "So, what happened?"

"My publisher killed the Vincent Louis story."

"No way! Why?" I was aghast. The newspaper's silence would be seen as a signal to lay off. It could bring our Louis investigation to a dead halt.

"Hope threatened my boss."

"The naked abuse of raw power?"

"Of course not," Donna said. "Jim Guthrie has been publisher a long time. He's no patsy. After the funeral, Hope invited him to dinner . . ."

"She's already on the make?"

"No, it wasn't like that, it was all very public. At Amici's."

That was a popular chichi joint I always meant to go to, but somehow never had. Even the conventioneers had heard of it by now, which meant it wouldn't be hip for long.

I asked, "How'd Hope lower the boom?"

"Craftily," Donna said. "She told Jim that acquaintances at the *Intruder* had tipped her that the tabloid was starting to look into allegations of tax evasion amongst VIPs living in resort areas."

"That must have been enough to cold cock him."

Donna assured me, "It wasn't. When Jim didn't roll over and play dead, Hope got serious."

"To people in your boss' bracket, what could be worse than an audit?" I asked. "I mean, besides what happened to Louis?"

"Blackmail."

"Whoa! Blackmail?" I said. "But who?"

"Jim's wife."

"That's playing dirty." I'd expect nothing less.

I knew Barbara Guthrie was a sixtyish, pixieish strawberry blonde with upwardly tilted green eyes and collagened frost pink lips. I could still see how pretty and pert she must have been as a girl. She was big on the Island charity circuit and enjoyed public speaking—about herself. Since Barbara was married to the publisher of the *Shiny Sheet*, people fought to get her to come to their parties.

Donna said, "Barbara came from Nowhere, North Carolina and

married a much older, very wealthy Island gentleman, and then embarked on a string of affairs."

Boy, that was a familiar litany. "That's not enough to interest the *Intruder*, unless Barbara was a Washington intern who slept with aliens," I said. "Two-headed topless aliens that looked like Elvis."

Donna snorted and added, "During one of Barbara's many 'encounters,' while she was going down on her lover in a pickup truck, her teenaged son followed with a rifle and shot him dead."

I almost choked on a cloying sugar-glazed strawberry. This was a juicy tidbit. Jim's wife had always struck me as being addicted to the applause she got for ponying up for worthy causes such as shrinks for the masses. I had always wondered why Pete, who got his social work start in Reno leading 12-step Gamblers Anonymous meetings, had never solicited Barbara Guthrie for a Palm Beach Crisis Center donation.

Anyway, at the end of every speech on her "life's journey to purity" and "spiritual perfection," Barbara Guthrie announced how her life won't be complete her wonderful son is married. There was always a strained silence and until now, I never knew why.

Hmmmm. I had to digest this as well as the pie. I had often wondered if Island big shots ever felt guilty and used philanthropy to assuage their consciences. Some of them reminded me of those dissolute British kings, who on their deathbeds staring Judgment Day in the face, directed the Royal treasury to build hospitals pronto.

"Good lord," I said. "No wonder Jim Guthrie folded like a deck of cards during Hurricane Andrew. The least Hope could do would be to pick up the 'tab.' Did she?"

"No. He did."

"Always the gentleman, isn't he?" I asked.

"Yeah. Jim has to protect his wife. I don't blame him for caving, but still . . . " Donna looked glumly at her plate of fish and chips. She had been around long enough to know *Shiny Sheet* stories get spiked, but other reporters, not hers. Until now.

"I'm not through with this," Donna said, with a steely look in her eye. "My boss just thinks I am."

"Oooh! Rebel with a cause. I like your attitude."

Not that I knew what we were going to do about it. I finished the last of my pie, which should have had more whipped cream. I would have to start eating more healthy or one day I would be sumo wrestling with Connie Favre. Throw in some creamed corn and Pete would be most appreciative. I patted my lips delicately with a linen napkin. Appearances must be observed.

I said with great significance, "Much as I would like to chat with you Donna, I do have a job to attend to."

"Really?"

"Yes, I must prepare for tonight's monthly board meeting. If not, everyone will be so disappointed."

Donna smirked, "Don't let the door hit you on your way out."

Chapter 15

THE CREW WITHOUT A CLUE

"*D*id the police catch the guy yet?"

"It didn't take long for Brenda to put the house up for sale."

"She won't be able to unload the place for what she paid for it."

"Brenda will sell to a German or Canadian. They won't know until it's too late."

"Hope was so calm at the funeral."

"What a lady. She was serene."

"Guess it hasn't hit her yet."

The Palm Beach Crisis Center board members were obsessed by the murder of Vincent Louis. I wasn't sure any agency business would get discussed tonight.

Felicia had volunteered to stay late and do the minutes at tonight's meeting. Before I could take a chair next to her, Pamela Wayne, one of the board members, whispered urgently, "What does he see in her?"

"Who?"

Pamela gestured at Pete, and then glanced at Connie, who sat as far away from him as possible, not letting on that in an hour she was going to meet her demon lover for a quickie at the Hampton Inn off Palm Beach Lakes Boulevard and I-95.

"What does he see in her?" Pamela asked. I pretended not to understand because it was safer that way.

"Does his wife know?" she persisted. Pamela's money was from owning a property insurance company with her husband. Even after 10 years in Palm Beach she was still a little rough around the edges. Her vices were smoking and lewd gossip at inappropriate times.

Instead of answering, I shook my head.

"You know something, Justine?" Pamela rasped loudly.

"What, Pamela?" I wished she'd modulate her raspy voice.

"You don't shit where you eat."

"Words to live by," I said.

She chuckled.

"Let us open with a prayer for the deceased," the Palm Beach Crisis Center president said, as we all bowed our heads in memory of the Mafioso Tabloid King. One of the ministers on our board said a few words.

"Isn't that sweet, considering we're going to be cheated out of $10 million?" Felicia muttered. She didn't have to be afraid anyone on the board would react, some of them were deaf due to age, others by choice. They ignored whatever they didn't want to hear. I thought of our board as the Crew Without a Clue.

The president asked Pete, "When do you expect the widow Louis will send the first installment?"

I glanced sharply at Felicia. It appeared Pete hadn't told the Crisis Center leader that Hope had reneged on the $10 million but had arranged for us to get her pets into Freudian analysis.

Felicia shook her head and hissed how she'd like to castrate

Vincent with a rusty fork. I was the only one to hear. Yes, Vincent planned to publish dirty photos of Felicia and her ex-lover, but I never thought for a moment she was behind his murder. I figured Felicia would pay someone to buy or steal the photos back. Maybe she would have asked Manny to rough up Vincent. But she seemed so angry at him, even in death. I didn't know what to think.

Pete answered the Crisis Center president, "I think Mrs. Louis' payment schedule may be delayed due to unforeseen circumstances."

"Of course," the president said, pretending to understand.

"How much of a delay?" Pamela gruffly asked.

"It is too early to broach the subject at this delicate time. We must not intrude upon the widow during her time of grief," Pete said. "We must be sensitive to her needs and should wait until a decent interval has passed."

"Oh," the president said.

Felicia grimaced. Pete so dominated the board that was supposed to oversee him; he even chose his own auditors, who reported to him, not the board. I knew he would be able to keep the Hope Baylor Louis kiss off secret until he had time to regroup. But what would happen six months from now when someone on the Crisis Center board might remember we were owed $10 million?

"Any questions?" the president said.

There were none.

"Let's move on to other business," he said. "OK. It's time for the Budget Committee report."

The treasurer chuckled and pantomimed passing the buck as did several other board members. Then he shrugged and had Pete "report" on the budget.

"We are doing quite well this month in receivables. I think by next quarter we will see improvement," Pete said soothingly. Just this morning he told staff we had so many bad debts to write off that he was cutting leave and considering layoffs.

"Let's proceed to new business," the president said and the board heard more Peter Pignatelli pablum. One director whispered about who Brenda had hired to drain her swimming pool. Another looked at his watch and said he didn't want to miss the game.

"Meeting adjourned."

The Crew Without a Clue had definitely missed the game . . . again.

Chapter 16

A CROSS TO BEAR

"*D*on't call them rich bitches," Dr. Michael Lavelle ordered the Palm Beach Crisis Center staff.

Dr. Mike, as the Island ladies called him, lead the Support Group for the Wealthy in Palm Beach. He had five advanced degrees and made $27 an hour with no benefits. The real money came from reassuring the wealthy of their victim status, so they weren't guilty about hoarding money. He ran seminars on "Compulsive Shopping Disorder: The Rising Crisis" and "The Worried Wealthy: Removing the Burden of Money."

Any day now, I expected him to get a lucrative book contract based on his article in the *Robb Report*, "Wealth Management."

"With wealth comes requests for charitable donations. It is impractical to say yes to every solicitation, but it is possible to say no without harming your reputation or troubling your conscience," Dr. Mike wrote. His article appeared between "an exclusive preview of some of the most desirable art and antiquities" for sale and "what could be better than owning your own jet?"

Felicia had been kidding me about this three-mile southern section of the 15-mile long, half a mile wide, narrow barrier Island. This neighborhood, instead of being filled with individual homes, was colonized by huge high rises on lush grounds, filled with magnificently appointed condos. However, because these unfortunates in the town of South Palm Beach (pop. 1,300) didn't have backyards and condos are less distinguished than detached homes, we were in slumville. The residents moved here well after land prices had gone crazy.

Donna warned me over lunch at Testa's that at this support group I would run into "snobbier than thou" types.

"As soon as these people meet, they sniff out each other's addresses."

"What's the big deal?" I asked, "They all live on the Island."

"Surely you jest," Donna said. "Some buildings are more desirable than others." She explained the further south someone lived, especially on Sloan's Curve, the less respect they got from their betters.

Before Dr. Mike opened the meeting, the ladies chatted over coffee. "Are you going to the American Heart Association gala committee meeting later this afternoon at Susan Pritchett's?" one woman asked her friend.

"No. I've already seen her home."

"I've never been and I was thinking of going," said another woman. "Is she ocean or lakefront?"

"Lakefront."

"Oh, that's not good. What about her art collection?"

"Reproductions."

"I think I'll relax at the pool instead."

This morning, I didn't know where I was on the Island slumometer, but the Support Group for the Wealthy was being hosted in a 4,000-square foot penthouse with ocean and Intracoastal views.

What a dump.

"Welcome to the Support Group for the Worthy," Dr. Mike said, and quickly covered. "I'm sorry, that was a slip of the tongue."

"A Freudian slip?" one of the ladies said.

We laughed. Arrayed like a pastel rainbow on a huge square U-shaped white leather couch in front of Dr. Mike, we were a veritable advertisement for casual, yet elegant, resort wear. After all, isn't therapy a form of very expensive leisure?

To fit in, I wore a pastel pink sleeveless vest with matching pants. And sandals. And purse. All the same perfect petal shade. Bought new, I might add. Matchy matchy may be despised in the northeast, but in Palm Beach it's de rigueur. People want to signal their rivals they can afford the entire outfit, so mix and match separates bought on different occasions are seen as low class. Of course, I bought my outfit over the course of three years.

Plus Felicia had warned me the day before, "For God's sake, whatever you do, don't wear your navy blazer."

"Why not?"

"On the Island that blazer will be the kiss of death. It labels you as someone who works for a living."

"Heaven forbid."

"Look Justine, you're being sarcastic, but you don't want to be seen as a low life. You'll thank me tomorrow. People who wear business suits to someone's home in Palm Beach look like they're trying way too hard. It also looks like they don't have much of a wardrobe. Where did you get that jacket anyway? From the Church Mouse?"

"No! I bought it new!" I was still a little sensitive about the Louis funeral.

Felicia explained the darker and more understated the jacket, the bigger the stigma. She instructed, "You must look silky, leisurely and ready for high tea in Bermuda."

"I promise to wash my hair and shave my legs," I assured her.

But even with Felicia's advice, I did not make the cut. I could tell by the sharp assessment I was given when I came into the room. Even my camera and notepad, which stimulate excitement in ordinary mortals, had no affect on these broads.

Felicia was wearing a fabulous canary yellow ensemble trimmed with black piping, with matching chapeau, (it wouldn't have occurred to me to find a pink hat), and she looked great. "Hey Mellow Yellow," I said as she waved. We grinned. She was in a much better mood today then she had been last night. Here she was among her own kind.

I wonder if it was my toes? My pink sandals revealed I did not have a pedicure, as every other woman did. My toenails lacked polish, as did the rest of me, I guess. The thing is, a lot of these old biddies get their toenails done because their feet are ugly. Some of them even have fungus and warts and stuff. My bare toenails were pink, smooth and healthy. Don't hate me because I am fungus free.

Oh, who was I kidding? I was marked by my lack of jewelry. These ditzes didn't care about my feet; they wanted to know if I had someone who could foot the bill.

Or was it my facial expression? I had smiled when I came in and greeted the hostess. That meant I was eager to please, not disdainful and haughty.

Really, why was I rejected and so fast? I'd solve the Louis murder first.

Dr. Mike had arrived. The women didn't know it, but early in his career he had locked down what they used to call homicidal maniacs in what used to be insane asylums. One time at the Big House, a raving lunatic got free and rammed Dr. Mike's head against the wall, until attendants came and restrained the madman. So jolly and sympathetic as he appeared, Mike did not intimidate easily.

"Is it true you're going to start charging us for these sessions?" one of the women asked.

"You're supposed to help people," another said accusingly.

"We do plan to start asking for fees, yes," Dr. Mike said.

"I heard you're going to ask us for $10."

"For every session?" one woman asked. "Or for the year?"

"The fee will be $5 and it will be per session," Dr. Mike said.

The women strenuously objected.

"Let's move on," Dr. Mike said. "I know we have other issues here. What should we discuss today?"

"The perils of shopaholism," one woman called out.

"How ordinary people do not realize that the rich also have problems."

"Such as?" Dr. Mike asked.

"Taxes."

"How sometimes you don't know if someone likes you for yourself."

"Reducing the intangibles tax on stocks and bonds."

"Getting jaded."

"Spoiled kids."

"Repealing the estate tax."

"Repealing the capital gains tax."

"How hard it is to find good help!" Everyone burst out laughing, including Dr. Mike.

The women respected Dr. Mike for being male. They were also gratified at the attentions and ministrations of a PhD with multiple degrees in mental health and counseling. And the ladies wanted to ply Dr. Mike for free advice after the meeting.

One battle ax preened what looked to be a 20-carat sapphire against her beige linen lap. "And to think these meetings don't cost us a thing!"

Chapter 17

FIT FOR ROYALTY

After an hour, the maids set up a yummy buffet of deli antipasto and vegetable platters with warm, crusty French bread. It beat a tray of frozen Costco cookies.

While serving myself melted brie on crunchy rosemary and sesame crackers, a woman separated from the crowd and introduced herself.

"You must be Justine, I'm Felicia's mother, Danielle Harold."

"Oh, I'm delighted to meet you. You must be so proud of your daughter," I said.

"Yes, I am, very," she beamed. "It hasn't been easy for Felicia."

"Well, she's doing the most wonderful job at Palm Beach Crisis Center. We all appreciate her so much."

"It isn't easy for someone who grew up in Felicia's circumstances to get by on her greatly reduced income," Mrs. Harold said.

I was puzzled.

She smiled, "I know, I know what this group is all about, but

Felicia is accustomed to nice things."

"Of course," I said. I still didn't get it.

"Her father calls her a 'glorified gopher.'"

I was insulted on Felicia's behalf. "You must be joking."

"No. I wish I were."

"You're serious?" I started to laugh, but Mrs. Harold looked sad. Why did Felicia's father despise her for doing honest labor?

"Felicia is on the go all day, but she is doing very important work for Palm Beach Crisis Center," I said.

Danielle Harold seemed to appreciate hearing that. "I'm just praying for the day when Felicia's estranged father forgives her and restores her income."

I smiled encouragingly; what could I say? I offered my hand.

"It was nice meeting you, Mrs. Harold. I hope to see you again sometime."

"Thank you, my dear. Will we be seeing you at any more of these meetings?"

"I don't think so. I'm not qualified."

She smiled. What was that little exchange all about? Felicia was living on a Palm Beach Crisis Center salary for employees not sleeping with Pete, so that meant it wasn't a living wage. It was a J.O.B., "Just Over Broke." I assumed Felicia made less than I, although with Pete you never knew, yet she traipsed in with a brand new designer outfit every day. And she was feeding a hungry mechanic, who was very physically active.

I concluded Felicia's mom meant she was secretly subsidizing Felicia, and was keeping snobby Daddy in the dark.

It was time for seconds and since the socialites knew I wasn't one of them, I would fill up. I could go for some more cheese and crackers—which they called "Italian flatbread." At the trough, I mean the buffet, I heard the ladies talk about local issues, especially the lack of mass transit in the county.

"But how are our servants going to get to our homes if the county cuts the Palm Beach bus route?" Danielle Harold asked.

"City Hall in West Palm want our buses freed up for busier streets," a woman said.

"You didn't hear this from me," a lady in pale lavender silk said, "But my husband had lunch with the head of the state's Department of Transportation. On the Island, Palm Tran buses will be reduced from once an hour to every two hours."

"Does that mean we have to chauffeur our own chauffeurs?" asked the hostess, to some chuckles.

"It forces us to be more flexible with our servants' schedules," Mrs. Harold said. "This is such an inconvenience." She told the hostess she had another meeting, then left.

"I heard you say you were from the Palm Beach Crisis Center?" a lady in white linen with moonstone necklace asked me.

"Yes."

"Well, I saw your ad in the paper that you sell used cars. I don't plan to be inconvenienced by the vagaries of the county bureaucracy; I want to buy a car for my upstairs maid."

She turned to her friend with a knowing look. "Just yesterday Mirta broached me about a pension."

"We had a '93 Pontiac Sunbird come in yesterday," I said.

"That's too new; do you have anything older, but reliable?"

Before I could answer, a woman in peach brocade said, "I just donated an '87 Toyota Camry to the Crisis Center. I warn you, my teenager used it for practice and now he's ready for the Mercedes." She turned to the woman in moonstone gems.

"If I had known you wanted a used car, I would have sold it to you directly."

Moonstone turned to me, "How much is the Camry?"

"Let me check," I said, and went out to the balcony where Felicia was enjoying the ocean breezes and having tea with her friends. She wasn't as excited as she usually was about making a sale.

"Who wants to know?" she asked.

"The lady with the moonstone jewelry," I said. "I don't know her name. What difference does it make?"

Felicia hesitated, then her usual salesmanship kicked in. "We'll sell it to her for $1,500."

I came back inside and reported the price, "$1,500."

"What?" shrieked the owner of the Camry. "Your agency just sent me a thank you letter bragging about the free towing and saying I could deduct $750. Just what is going on here? I'm going to give Hope Louis a piece of my mind!"

The other women surrounded me and glared as if I were to personally blame for the car foul up. That's the last time I would try to sell used cars for our charity. I said, "Mrs. Louis had nothing to do with the purchase of your used car."

"No, but pretty soon she's going to be your boss and Hope better know about your gross ineptitude," said Camry woman, red faced and indignant. "When I finally find out what's going on over there, start looking for another job."

I let her rant. I had worked in Palm Beach long enough to know that trying to placate people who throw their weight around only encourages them to be more despotic. I was relieved when after an awkward silence the women began chatting about Princess Diana.

The hostess mentioned Donna's column in today's *Shiny Sheet* about how to comport yourself with royalty. "I'm clipping this article so I don't embarrass myself," she said. "Donna tells you when to bob your head and not curtsy. And don't say, 'My Grace.'"

"Princess Michael of Kent will insist upon it," said her friend, "At least she did when I had her for brunch two years ago. Her staff instructed me to refer to her as Ma'am, and she doesn't care how much you're worth."

"I don't want to go overboard with these people. Some of my friends say 'Your Royal Highness' when all that is called for is 'Sir.'"

"I heard you shouldn't make such a big deal over greeting a garden variety baronet—they are as common as dirt!"

"Not quite."

"Hope Louis told me you can't assume all dukes are royal. They aren't."

Hope had said that? Now we were getting somewhere. I tried to be inconspicuous.

"Yes, Hope told me that 20% of the nonroyal dukes descend from acknowledged bastards of Charles II, also known as the Merry Monarch."

"Well, the Merry Widow should know."

Snickers.

"Did you hear Hope will be in France this summer?" asked our hostess.

"Is she going to forget?"

"I don't think so. She's going to buy real estate. I hear she's going to check out castles for sale in Italy and France."

"What does she have against England?"

"She says she can't maintain any privacy there because Fleet Street is full of yellow journalists."

"Well, it takes one to know one."

There were more snickers here than at the candy counter.

"I'm serious. Christie's has put Hope in touch with an 83-year-old contessa who needs to unload her 17th-century castle, built on Roman ruins. You should see the gardens there. She's hoping to sell it for $10 million to a rich American."

"Why is the old lady selling?" asked Letitia van Anders.

"The contessa's got a liquidity problem; all of these aristocrats always do," said our hostess. She looked elegant, was dressed all in white, with heavy gold jewelry.

"Now that Vincent is gone, our Hope is planning to re-invent herself again." They laughed snidely. So it was possible those Vegas chorus girl rumors were true? Or were these women referring to Hope's first husband who picked her up in Akron, when she would have been thrilled with $65,000 . . . for the whole year.

"Hope has been answering the ads in the back of the *Wall Street Journal* and The Economist about titles for sale. The ads claim if you buy a title, you are guaranteed 'priority' on the social list of Queen Elizabeth II. Hope won't set foot in Great Britain, unless it's as a

Marquessa."

"I thought all she read was W," van Anders said.

"And the *Shiny Sheet*," Camry Woman said.

"You mean she only reads the *National Intruder*!"

The hostess said, "You're both wrong. The fake nobility ads are in *Town & Country*, and in any case, Hope wouldn't buy a title from the back of a magazine. It's not like she needs the discount. She's already paid $1,000 for *Burke's Peerage* to find her a French title. Between you, me and the wall, she's willing to pay between $47,000 to $110,000 with an acre or two thrown in. She's after one of the most distinguished French titles, so she can get a coat of arms."

"And that's without a chateau," van Anders said.

"Hope will pay *Burke's* an additional fee for the L'Intruder coat of arms," the hostess explained.

"I guess if Trump can invent a coat of arms, so can Hope Louis."

"She'll use the *Intruder* logo: an eyeball peering through a keyhole."

"The family motto will be, 'Intruding Minds Want to Know.' In Latin."

Pig latin would suit her better, but something didn't sound kosher.

"Isn't it impossible for Mrs. Louis to become a French aristocrat?" I asked. They looked at me like I was the proverbial village idiot.

I plowed in, "What about the French Revolution?"

"Absolutely irrelevant!" one woman said. She seemed astonished that I was still there.

Lavender Silk explained, "*Burke's* researches the archives back until 1789 and finds who owned land back then. It is the land that carries the title."

"The title doesn't come from the families who once owned the land?" I asked.

"That is correct," our hostess said. "If an American buys the right piece of land which comes with the right paperwork, he can be transformed into a baron, a count, even a marquis."

"So it doesn't matter that the title to the land was granted by a monarchy that was thrown out over 200 years ago?" I persisted.

The women shook their heads with disgust, either because I was tasteless, or dimwitted, or both. The aristocrats who had once owned the land had met their fate at the guillotine. Let them eat cake!

I wondered what was for dessert?

Though the women were mocking Hope, they knew if anyone could pull off the grand scheme, she could. Hope had the cash, the determination, the French couture and the Countess Collagen looks.

Felicia had wandered back inside for some fruit and appeared fascinated by Hope's new social goal.

"Hope learned French when attending fashion shows in Paris and it certainly will come in handy in her new life as Marie Antoinette. Croissant, anyone?"

Chapter 18

ROGUES GALLERY

Once I was back in the car and put in a CD from the rock group Offspring (I didn't have any Maurice Chevalier), I called Donna.

"Society."

"Well, it looks like you've got your Support Group for the Wealthy story. I'll write it up later today and e-mail it with the photos."

"How'd it go?"

"It was everything I thought it would be."

"That bad?"

"Yep."

"How were the women?"

"Do the words 'self absorbed' mean anything to you?"

"Naaaaaaw," Donna said, very sarcastic, "I never come across that covering charity galas at the *Shiny Sheet*."

"Well, the meeting had its uses," I admitted. "It turns out Hope is going to be the next Madame Pompadour."

I filled in Donna on Hope's plans to buy a chateau and be the Countess of Monte Cristo. She wasn't surprised.

"Buying a title is practically a career move for these dames," she said. "But I'm glad you told me; that explains why Hope plans to announce she is back in circulation by hosting a fund raiser for the Friends of Versailles."

Donna paused. "At least she buried him first."

"Oui, oui, mademoiselle," I said in an atrocious accent.

"Are you going after the reward?" Donna asked.

"What reward?" Nothing like being the last to know.

"Hope has just issued a $1 million reward for information leading to the arrest and conviction for the murder of her late husband. The last six people I've talked to say Hope realizes that she doesn't appear grief stricken and this would restore her reputation as loving wife."

I thought about it. "I find it hard to take the offer seriously."

"Why not?" Donna asked. "She's got the money."

I wasn't so sure of that. "I'm a rank amateur at this sort of thing. Some professional will break the case before I do."

"But you're following every Louis lead that comes your way."

That was true. Sometime, when I was less frenzied, I would have to sit down and figure out why this case was so important to me. "Hold on, Donna, I'm being paged." It was the Palm Beach Crisis Center receptionist.

"Justine?"

"Yeah?"

"Pete told me to page you; you've got an emergency meeting at Combined Charities in 30 minutes. Haul ass."

Sacre bleu, should my delicate ears be exposed to such vulgarity?

"OK. I'm on my way."

I started the car, picked up my cell and returned to Donna.

"I've been summoned and I can't talk and drive at the same time. I'll get back to you later today. And Donna?"

"Yes?"

"Au revoir, mon petite."

Pete looked nervous at our command performance before our main benefactor, Combined Charities, which called the shots at Palm Beach Crisis Center. Downstairs, Pete was Emperor with consort. Upstairs he was just another flunky with his hand out before the Combined Charities board of directors.

The Crisis Center's lower status was reflected in our schizo building. We even had two lobbies. Combined Charities welcomed potential donors with a lavish marble lobby with gold leafed contributors' names plastered everywhere. There were vases of fresh flowers and a couple of Old Masterish looking oil paintings. The Crisis Center had a scratched, plastic coffee table on shabby carpet festooned by dusty artificial flowers and plastic shepherdess statuettes with chipped paint.

Combined Charities was the prestige, powerhouse board of Palm Beach. It had the strict rule, "Give, Get or Get Off." Board members either gave $100,000 a year, raised it, or left the board. You didn't join in the first place unless you were a zillionaire or connected to one. That meant besides the usual heirs and gold diggers and until recently, a Tabloid King, there were a lot of crafty tax dodgers, union busters, sweatshop owners (domestic and foreign), law firm partners and slumlords.

I recognized Richard M. Schlesinger, who runs more than 20 housing projects nationwide. He'd paid about $2 million in fines for "misuse" of housing funds, code violations and failure to pay utility bills. He never met a federal rent subsidy he didn't like and lives on 2.5 acres in an eight-bedroom oceanfront mansion.

Bill Koch, the oil heir and *Forbes 400* listee worth $650 million, was also on board. Koch got American taxpayers to subsidize his 1992 America's Cup win, in part by turning his $68.5 million yachting syndicate into a tax-exempt foundation.

However, this Rogue's Gallery had some standards. It turned

down part-time Island resident Larry Flynt while courting people of a higher caliber such as Christopher Reeve's pal and heavy duty philanthropist Lois Pope and the county's best known lawyer, Bob Montgomery. Their neighbors Brenda Ecklund and Hope Louis were also directors, though neither were attending today.

Danielle Harold had already taken an ornate leather chair with brass rivets and carved oaken armrests. As the board members refreshed themselves with snacks from TooJay's deli, Pete and I were waved to some folding chairs near the wall.

The last to arrive was Felicia who fussed about delivering some papers to Pete. I saw they were checks he and Connie Favre were co-signing. None was urgent so Felicia was apparently here on a pretext.

When Danielle Harold spotted her daughter, she delightedly waved her to take the seat next to hers. Maybe this is how Felicia reminded Pete of her family connections while she also persuaded her Mom that she's a dedicated nonprofit employee. I had to admit Felicia looked like she belonged with the third or fourth trophy wives of the grandsons of long dead robber barons—who passed for Island aristocracy.

Be they gold digger or white collar criminal, they all pulled in the dough for Combined Charities from a very tight network of friends and peers, who were honored with a strict, tiered system of parties. The more they gave, the more elaborate the party with A-list celebrities, famous authors and guest speakers. Today the Combined Charities board was atwitter about the most exclusive party yet, to be held at Le Soleil, a 40,000-square-foot private home that had never hosted a charity event before.

"How much are we charging for this thing?"

"It will be an additional $50,000 above our annual contribution, plus the $400 per person cover."

"Have you heard Celine Dion will be giving a private concert?"

"Yeah, but $400? Isn't that ridiculous on top of $50,000?"

"That way you cover the cost of the party."

"For that kind of money, I'm going to bring additional guests."

Combined Charities had an exclusive women's club, the "Proud Peacocks of Palm Beach" who wore dazzling gold brooches studded with gems, in the shape of the bird displaying full plumage. Very NBC.

The pins advertised exactly how much the women had given at a glance. For instance, a plain gold pin with no gems meant you had given an initial $100,000. The sapphire eyes were each worth an additional $25,000. Ruby beak, another $10,000; emeralds on the tail feathers, each another $45,000; pearl claws, diamonds on the breast, ka-ching! The social cachet was priceless.

Maybe some people would think this sounds corny but you can't be too obvious on the Island. The Peacocks, avian and human, meant that Combined Charities pulled in $25 million a year. And every Christmas, Combined Charities ordered its staff to take up a collection to give the overworked Colombian janitor a bonus.

Danielle Harold turned to Proud Peacock Kathleen DuRoss Ford, the widow of Henry Ford II, with annual bequest of $15 million. "Kathleen, I understand there was a lovely article about you in the paper."

Kathleen smiled modestly. When a 57-year-old woman and her sick 92-year-old mother lost their mobile home in a hurricane (smashed by a 40-foot banyan tree), Kathleen paid off the woman's new $8,000 trailer at the Happy Landings trailer park. The woman, who made $250 a week cleaning offices at night, was ecstatic.

What Mrs. Harold didn't mention was that Ford had reneged on a $1 million reward promised on America's Most Wanted for the recovery of her $15 million in uninsured, stolen jewels. She had been cleaned out of everything, but her Proud Peacock. Apparently the burglars thought it was too garish to be real and left it behind.

Three Georgia jewelers cracked the case and helped with a sting, two of them against an armed man. Ford's personal lawyer told the jewelers Ford would pay the reward but it never happened. The jewelers sued Ford who keeps stalling and one of them died of cancer at age 46.

The *Post* put Ford's $8,000 gift on the front page.

Chapter 19

PET CAUSE

"*D*anielle," Kathleen DuRoss Ford said, "You must be very proud of how hard your daughter works for charity." Mrs. Harold beamed and Felicia smiled modestly as Combined Charities Executive Director Lloyd Biggs convened the meeting.

"Ladies and gentlemen, I've called this meeting because we need a game plan during the current crisis with the death of Vincent Louis. His demise could not have come at a worse time. Every year the competition we face gets tougher. Right now there are 42 nonprofits, the barbarians at the gates, trying to raise $360 million from the 10,000 residents of Palm Beach."

"They all keep going to the same well," Koch said.

"As well they should, since two dozen of our neighbors are on the *Forbes 400*," Danielle Harold said. "And don't forget the other two dozen elsewhere in the county."

Biggins said, "These nonprofits are after anyone with spare

change; they aren't just targeting the *Forbes 400*. They are soliciting from potential donors with a net worth of just $5 million."

"Those aren't very deep pockets," Ford said.

"That's true, but from our rivals' perspective when they target Palm Beach, they have a good chance of reaching some of the 483,000 Americans who are worth a minimum of $5 million. That beats wasting time with the total U. S. population of 287 million. In the coming years even more charities will converge on our affluent Island," Biggins said.

He added, "These times demand not only that we dig deeper in our wallets, but invent ways to bring qualified donors into our fold and keep them within the Combined family."

Biggins turned to Pete. "Pete, we called you here to see what you could do about this."

Before Pete could formulate an answer Biggins specified, "Specifically, what can we do about consoling Hope during this terrible time of shock and bereavement? She is very special to all of us."

Maybe they should give her a title and a chateau? That would work.

As soon as Pete opened his mouth, Lloyd cut him off. "I'm not asking for suggestions," he said brusquely, enjoying making Pete squirm. "I'm instructing you that the Combined Charities board of directors has decided to console Hope and attract future high income donors by creating a glossy new magazine, Palm Beach Society Pets."

Pete blinked. His eyes were kind of red and had bags. He lowered his face and rubbed them with one hand. Was it my imagination or was the other hand in his lap starting to shake? Meanwhile I knew I'd be doing this assignment and I'm wondering what do I look like: Justine Romanoff, Palm Beach Pet Detective?

Lloyd Biggins continued, "This is an easy way to court a potential major donor. We're aware Vincent never had a chance to write you the first check of the promised $10 million. With this magazine, we will embrace his widow, keep her in our fold and when the time is appropriate, remind Hope of her obligation."

"I'm not a magazine publisher," Pete said. That was unlike him to let his temper flare, in this crowd, even though what he said made sense. Well, the last few days had been stressful for everyone at Palm Beach Crisis Center.

But here's the shocker: you mean to tell me this group of high rollers didn't know Hope had reneged? I knew the dopey Crisis Center board would be clueless until Pete chose to enlighten them, if ever. But this was a flock of savvy and savage Peacocks.

Dora Reynolds, the cigarette heiress, spoke up. "We envision a chronicle of the superlative measures to which people on the Island will go to pamper their pets."

Pete looked like he wanted to be sick. I'm sure he thought his face was its usual mask. "You're aware Hope is having us do pet therapy."

"Yes, I am," Dora said. "I'm the one who suggested it to her." She added, "I would love to see features on catered pet birthday parties and the latest pet fashions, and . . . " her eyes sparkled, " . . . pictures of pet owners."

Kathleen Ford said, "Of course, Hope Louis will be on the cover of the first issue."

"Of course," Pete said as Lloyd smirked. Pete knew when to fold.

Dora said, "I hereby reserve a page for Mr. Tibbs."

"Who?"

"That's the kitty I got for my housekeeper."

"Dora," Kathleen said, shocked, "You can't put in pets owned by the help. This is going to be an elegant, high class magazine."

"Oh, I should have been more clear," Dora said, "I want two pages for me and my five cats, and one for Mr. Tibbs."

Ford smiled.

"Mrs. Renal," Pete began.

"Reynolds!" she reprimanded.

Pete tried again. "Mrs. Reynolds, it is going to be very expensive to publish this *Pet Society Celebration*."

"*Palm Beach Society Pets*," attorney Monty Robbins corrected.

"How are we going to pay for this?" Pete asked.

"Peter," Dora Reynolds said, annoyance entering into her

scrawny, high-pitched voice, "This magazine will not only pay for itself, but it will make us a fortune. Not only will we attract donors, but they will pay a premium to be in these pages. We all know Palm Beachers take better care of their pets than their kids."

Knowing laughter. There was a persistent Island rumor about Monty, that to discipline his drug addled son, he tethered him to his car and made him run behind him.

Hard to believe someone would do that to their dog.

"My three cats are the best children I have ever had," said Priscilla Morgan, the mouthwash heiress (family fortune made by falsely claiming that its mouthwash prevents colds). Everyone smiled.

Lloyd added, "We will distribute the magazine all over the Island."

Was it me, or was this starting to make sense? Combined Charities had already run the numbers: print run of 5,000, readership of 20,000. Income from subscriptions, newsstand sales and best of all: the Islanders would supply the photos and most of the text and then pay to have it all run in the magazine at $2,500 per page. These people can't get enough of seeing their own mugs—which sometimes resembled those of their pets.

"Eventually, we may even go hardcover," Lloyd said.

"And don't forget advertising," Priscilla chirped. "Island jewelry stores sell diamond pendants for dogs and pearl necklaces for cats."

"What about equine photography?" Monty asked.

"They shoot horses, don't they?" Priscilla asked. "I don't know about jewelry for horses, leather accessories, maybe?"

I was waiting for some woman to say that her three stallions made the best husbands she ever had, but where's Catherine the Great when you need her?

"We'll include annual 'Bow Wow and Meow' awards!"

"And we'll have to make sure to cover special Island pet events, such as weddings, the Halloween party at the Island Pet Hospital and the April black-tie gala, Coats and Tails."

Pete and I looked at each other. Diamond-studded black tie gala? For cats and dogs?

As great as this sounded for Combined Charities, this was small potatoes for what the widow Hope had in mind. She planned to conquer the Continent, or at least Paris. This magazine wouldn't sway her even if we put her in the centerfold with a French poodle.

Holding a French poodle, I mean.

Now that Hope was taken care of, Eleanor Hecht, who was always all business, sternly turned to Pete.

"Pete, while we have you here, I feel we should address some serious issues. We've been looking at your budget. We feel that instead of paying people a stipend to visit isolated seniors in poor health, you should find volunteers who will go for free."

There was an uncomfortable pause. As ever, Pete was the master of self control. Palm Beach Crisis Center was supposed to find people to cook meals for the frail elderly, take them shopping and to the doctors, do light housekeeping and be lifesavers, for free. I could count on one hand the number of volunteers we had from the Island over the past five years who did this for clients, and have four fingers left over. And we were supposed to find people to do this who didn't need the money.

"That's certainly something I'll take up with the Palm Beach Crisis Center board," Pete said imperturbably.

"Well, make sure the board really has a chance to discuss it this time, Pete," said Lloyd. "They're the ones making the decisions. Supposedly."

There was no love lost between Pete Pignatelli and Lloyd Biggins, the man Pete tricked into hiring Connie so long ago, on the basis of her "productivity and wonderful communal work credentials." Well, she communed all right, but I think it was her proclivities Pete preferred, not her productivity. Biggins had it in for both of them ever since.

Biggins is what passed for a boss for Pete. He couldn't fire Pete—only the Palm Beach Crisis Center board could void his contract—but he could yank his chain.

They had never gotten along. Pete's resentment grew after Biggins blackballed him with Bernie Madoff, a fellow Palm Beach Country Club member who golfed with most of the Crew Without a Clue. Half our board was in with Bernie and the other half pretended they were. Pete had inquired about investing once. Madoff rejected him for being insignificant and had Biggins relay the message.

So today, when Lloyd Biggins told us pets are our new priority and that we must make Hope happy, we hear and we obey. Sometimes I felt sorry for Pete.

Though we were dissed and dismissed, Lloyd kept Pete sitting there just to show he could. Once the agenda was covered, the Combined Charities board started discussing Palm Beach County's proposed "living wage."

"What a load of crap," said Marvin Wolf, a CEO who made $34,000 a day. "It's no one's business what I pay my employees."

I wondered if he knew or cared that if minimum wage had grown at the same rate as his pay in the '90s, the guy who washed his cars would be earning $23 an hour.

However, Wolf's *Fortune 500* corporation had scored billions in tax rebates over the years; somehow it made more money after April 15!

Wolf said, "Today it's a county living wage proposal, tomorrow it will be a state income tax. The day Florida does that is the day I move out of here."

"Me too."

"Same here."

Lloyd Biggins said, "The state would never dare; the entire Island would evacuate."

Would that be so bad?

Chapter 20

A TAXING TASK

"Those guys make Vincent Louis look like an angel," I muttered to Felicia on the way downstairs to the Crisis Center.

Felicia shook her head. "I don't think so. My mother's board tries to do good. Louis may have been on the board at Combined Charities, but he never really belonged. He was a pig."

That was harsh. When I first started indulging my idle curiosity about the Louis murder I hadn't a clue it would have anything to do with where I worked. But strangely, the more I snooped around the Island, the more I kept coming back to my colleague, the sartorially impressive Felicia Harold. If I wanted to stay safe in the paranoid pressure cooker that was my job, I had to pretend I was an ignorant little automaton with nothing more serious on my mind than stupid pet tricks and promoting the greater glory of Peter Pignatelli.

My frustration and anxiety were almost enough to make me want to clean my desk. But not quite. I spent the rest of the day feverishly working up a pet magazine prototype.

When I got home after work, I was ready to crash. I waved to my neighbor from across the street, "Debbie Dior." She was walking back from the mailboxes on the corner.

"Justine, just look at this letter," she said, waving a piece of paper around. I saw a piece of Crisis Center letterhead.

"What's wrong?" After my embarrassment with Moonstone Lady and Camry Woman at the Support Group for the Wealthy, I hoped Debbie's letter didn't have to do with my having persuaded her and her husband to donate a $5,000 used car to our nonprofit. I had promised the write off would make it worth their while.

"This is my so-called 'tax deduction' letter from your so-called agency," Debbie said angrily. "Now I know why you'll always be a nonprofit."

She handed me the letter, written by Felicia and signed by Pete, thanking the couple for contributing a car worth – THUD — $2,500.

This was awful.

"Justine, I know this isn't your fault, but what's the deal here?" she asked indignantly. "The Blue Book says $5,000. No wonder your agency always has its hand out. You have incompetents selling donated cars for a lot less than they are worth!"

"No wonder I never get a raise," I said lamely, renewing my vow I would never get my friends involved with donating to Palm Beach Crisis Center again. Or I wouldn't have any friends. I knew the Diors' car was in good condition and figured the ever acquisitive Felicia must have goofed up. Maybe she was distracted by Manly Manny's many attentions.

"Listen Debbie," I said. "I'll see if there's something I can do. I'm really sorry about this."

The next morning I skulked over to the bookkeeping department and shut the door.

Lucette looked up, surprised. She didn't socialize much with the staff.

"Lucette?"

"Mmmmhmmmmm." Lucette had already gone back to her spreadsheet. She almost never took her eyes off the computer screen. The bookkeeper had been at the agency 15 years and worked non-stop. But because she didn't have a college degree and Pete wasn't attracted to her, she was repeatedly passed over for promotions.

There wasn't much of a future at Palm Beach Crisis Center for any of us, unless we serviced Pete. But without a degree, it was hopeless. After Lucette worked 10-hour days here, including unpaid overtime, she worked a second job at a hospital cafeteria. Her husband had been a construction worker but was out on disability. Lucette was trusted with a lot of confidential information and was unfortunately discreet and I wasn't sure she would speak to me. But she was the only one, besides Pete and Connie, who would have the goods.

"Lucette, could you help me figure out something?"

"I might."

I snuck a peek at the computer screen. More budget cuts looming.

I stalled. "How about a cigarette break?" I didn't smoke, But Lucette did and as far as I could tell, it was her only vice.

"Meet you outside by the gazebo," she said.

Keeping in James Bond mode, I left a few minutes after Lucette did. Normally, it wouldn't appear suspicious that the two of us would leave the building at the same time, but this whole Vincent Louis case was making me paranoid.

We met at a pile of falling down, rotting wooden boards, that had once been a pleasant gazebo. Now every remaining surface was covered with cigarette butts. Blech. Of course, for the kind of info Lucette had, I'd breathe in tar fumes.

The bookkeeper took a deep drag and blew out the smoke. She was the only staff person allowed to wear spandex leggings (so maybe she was a valued employee after all) and she piled a long, frowsy, pilled beige sweater on top. Her shoes were canvas pull-ons with worn rubber soles. Lucette regally gazed at the nearby drainage pond. She was not unaware of the drama of the situation, I sensed.

"What's up?" she asked.

I plunged in. "What's the story with the $5,000 car my neighbors just donated to the agency?" Weeks earlier, when I knew the Diors were going to come across, I had told Lucette to be on the look out.

"The $2,500 car you mean?" Somewhere in those flinty blue eyes of hers, I saw a glint of amusement.

"No," I said, "The $5,000 car."

Another drag. Then a long, lingering gaze. Lucette had short, slicked back black hair, shot through with gray. She wore dangly Christmas tree earrings. "Why do you want to know?"

"My neighbor let me have it last night. She's really teed off about this."

Lucette puffed some more. My lungs pulled in more nicotine. Then she revealed, "Your neighbors aren't the first."

"Aren't the first to what?"

"A few weeks ago, Felicia practically gave away a car that was donated to us." Lucette sounded annoyed.

"Gave away?" Hard nosed Felicia who knew the price of everything, be it a counterfeit Fendi from a black market Boca Raton garage, to the real deal on Worth Avenue?

Lucette continued, "One of the staffers here donated a 10-year-old Honda Civic. She specified the proceeds go to advertising her program so she could get more clients. It should have sold for . . . "

"Don't tell me. Twice as much as it went for?" I asked.

"Yes," Lucette said. "The car should have sold for $1,000. Instead, Felicia and Manny practically gave it away." I wasn't imagining things. The discrete bookkeeper was disgusted.

I asked, "How much?"

Had I scared her off? Something was bothering her so I softened my approach.

"What do you mean by 'gave it away?'"

"Five hundred dollars."

I was outraged. "For a CAR? Or do you mean a 10-speed?"

Lucette snickered. "When the staffer asked about it, Felicia said a lady had come to Manny saying she was out of work and needed a car to go to job interviews. Manny felt so sorry for her, so he sold the Honda for next to nothing."

"'Next to nothing' is right," I said.

Lucette almost, but not quite, snickered. It was almost like watching a cat laugh because it was about that rare. "I don't think Felicia feels sorry for anybody," she said, cryptically. "And she never gives anything away."

I shook my head. "You're not kidding."

I added, "I doubt any of the $500 went to promote the program." I would know, since I placed all agency ads.

"Mmmhmm. "I gotta get back inside," Lucette said as she put away her cigarettes.

I pulled out my cell phone. With the rotting gazebo as my new base of operations, even in the shade I was sweating in the hot, humid air, I called Donna at the *Shiny Sheet*.

"Society."

"Donna? Justine. I need a favor."

"The perfume and other gifts I got this week are locked up until Christmas—you know that."

"Not that kind of a favor," I said. "I need information."

"What did you have in mind?"

"Donna, I need you to check with your police sources; I'm starting to wonder about Manly Manny."

"No. He has not had any enlargement procedures; I checked with my best medical sources," Donna said, muffling a laugh.

"I'm not wondering about Manny's manliness; I want to know if he has a record."

"Manny? I didn't know he could sing. At the funeral he lacked a certain polish, but that's part of his appeal."

"Donna, I'm not kidding. Please check."

"Does this have anything to do with Vincent Louis?"

"Not really," I said.

"Well, all my spare time is going to the Vincent Louis case," Donna said.

"Even though Jim Guthrie said you're not allowed to run any stories on it?" I asked.

"I will eventually," Donna said with her usual confidence.

I said, "Maybe what I need to know is related . . . "

"How could that be?"

"It's possible," I said. "Please see if you can find out."

A few minutes later, when I had returned to my office and was waving my armpits under the air conditioning vent, Donna called back.

"Well Justine, your instincts were right. Our Latin Lover has a big list of priors . . . "

"You mean drug dealing?" I guessed.

"Yes."

She had something important, otherwise she wouldn't be dragging it out.

"And what else?" I asked.

"He's a violent offender."

I hadn't been expecting that. I know Felicia liked 'em wild and wooly, but that was crossing the line.

Donna continued, "Manuel Rodriguez fled Caracas after a gangster 'business partner' was found dead in an alley," Donna said.

"Manny shot him?" I asked.

"Not quite. He slipped and fell . . . "

"Oh. That's a relief."

" . . . On a knife. It went straight into his heart."

Gross. I shivered and hoped it wasn't true. "But here in West Palm, Manny's just a mechanic, servicing cars and Felicia."

Otherwise Manny was capable of murdering Vincent Louis for Felicia. She could pay him well, offering him the lush Palm Beach Crisis Center car selling franchise and her own body work.

Donna asked, "So how are the two connected?"

I knew she loved a good conspiracy, but at this point I didn't feel like I had enough to go on. I said, "I'm not sure yet." I knew it was lame when I said it but I needed to buy time.

The rest of the day I hid in my office, dodging Lucette, avoiding Felicia and praying Manny wouldn't stop by the building for one of his visits. It was getting late and it was time to go home and crash with a big bowl of old fashioned, oil-popped popcorn.

As I walked to my front door, I noticed some kind of note dangling from the doorknob. Not another pizza flyer. It would be one thing if you could get half off one pizza. Instead it was always, 'Buy one, get one free.' I wasn't THAT hungry.

But this was no junk flyer. It looked like a bizarre ransom note cobbled together with letters cut from different magazine articles, haphazard and threatening:

Kip Away

or U

will B

next !

I dropped it fast. This had to be related to the Louis case. My grubby paws had been all over this note. How could I give this to Sgt. Hajost?

I called the cops. I quickly placed the note in a plastic bag and shoved it on my kitchen counter. Even as I freaked that someone involved in the murder of Vincent Louis knew where I lived, a small part of me tried to stay cold and analytical. The 'KIP' looked deliberately misspelled, almost as if the writer was trying to look foreign, or uneducated.

Who did this? Manny? Felicia? The two of them in cahoots? Had Lucette said anything? She wasn't the type to let anything slip, but it was possible with all the stress she was under . . . Or had Donna traded the Manny chip with a cop, who had his own underworld sources?

By then, the police came and one of them immediately suggested next time, I use a paper bag to store evidence. Wearing gloves and using tweezers he carefully pulled the note out of the plastic bag, which I realized had been used to store onions and there was now some peel on the note. Methodically the policemen examined what I thought of as a death threat, then just as carefully, in a move that hadn't occurred to me, looked at the back of the note.

Which read, "Come over for subs and The Bachelorette. If you dare."

Omigod, that was Debbie Dior's hand writing. I'd recognize her red BIC and the plump little heart dotting the "i," anywhere. Just as I broke out in a sweat of acute humiliation and the cop and his buddy were staring at me strangely; there was a knock at the door.

"Justine, I'm really sorry." In walked Danny Dior. "I saw the police car outside. I'm the one who left the ransom note."

At the expression on my face, he said, "It was a practical joke. You didn't believe it, right? It was so stupid, no one would take it seriously." Well, that made me feel better. As Danny dug himself in deeper, the cop with the tweezers started to snicker, the other one shook his head and rolled his eyes. I felt like an idiot.

I hadn't told the Diors about my Vincent Louis murder investigation, but Debbie had told her husband how she chewed me out at the mail box over the Palm Beach Crisis Center tax deduction letter. Dan had said it wasn't my fault and Debbie wanted to make it up to me with dinner and reality TV. Ooops.

I apologized to the Palm Beach County sheriffs for wasting their time and tried to salvage their evening.

"Can I buy you guys some pizza?"

Chapter 21

THE GIFT OF GRAB

The Diors had been sweet tonight, but I didn't feel much better even after the hoagie sandwich and hokey show. I came home and collapsed on my bed. As I lay on my back and stared at the revolving ceiling fan, I kept thinking I had been missing something about Louis. All along I had been focusing on why so many people hated Louis—enough to want him dead—but what had been going on in Louis' head that could have brought about his murder?

He had been furious at the Palm Beach Crisis Center for sending out redundant gala invitations in his name to all his pals. He had chewed out Pete. He had not offered to pay for software that automatically removed redundant names, or "de-dupe," as we say in the mass mail biz. That's the Donor's Dilemma: it was easier to pledge $10 million to the betterment of humanity in the distant future, than pay $375 to fix a simple problem right now.

A few years back Louis had torn down an almost new $7 million mansion on his land because by Island standards it was small and old fashioned. Then he built a bigger, even more ostentatious home. Later he objected when the Crisis Center sent out too much bulk mail at 11 cents a piece.

Vincent had lectured Pete, who earned $175,000 annually, with lavish T&E expense account, agency-paid leased Lexus and $60,000 a year pension, plus all-expenses paid mistress, on fiscal prudence. Pete humbly listened and pretended to care as Louis carried on about wasting postage.

Of course, if Louis were still around he would be the first to tell us, "I earned my money. You beg for yours."

We will never have the guts to answer: "We charities apologize for our irritating and incessant begging, but you don't pay enough taxes to fund these programs through the government."

You say to us, "Be gone!" We say to you, "Beg On!"

I called Donna. I didn't usually bother her at home, knowing she'd welcome my gossip as part of her job when she was in the *Shiny Sheet* newsroom, but I had to talk. It was weird when she answered the phone, "Hello."

"Not 'Society?'" I said.

"Oh, I'm off duty now. I just came home from four different affairs."

"Wow! Does your husband know, you hussy?" I joked. I knew what she meant, but kidding her made me feel more like myself.

"Glen hates the party scene. He tells me to start without him," Donna said.

During Season, Donna had a lot of ground to cover; she stayed 20 minutes at each event, just long enough to make an appearance. Island hostesses showered her with gifts just for showing up.

"A Palm Beach society editor is never off duty," I said, trying to keep it light. But now Donna's antennae were on alert.

After a short pause, she asked, "What's wrong?"

"That depends how long you've got," I said.

Donna must have heard how tired I was. Before I could tell her my suspicions about Manny and Felicia, she listened patiently as I described my overreaction to the Diors' note and how they had every right to be disgusted with me and Palm Beach Crisis Center.

"That reminds me," Donna said. Tonight she had tumbled to the fact that Pete and Connie had been guests at the Louises, a few weeks before Louis submersed.

"You know that Pete and Connie weren't asked to stay for dinner?" she asked.

"How B-list," I said.

"You didn't know that Vincent had it in for Connie."

"You're kidding." I hadn't heard that. "You aren't suggesting Connie had something to do with his death?"

No way. Never. As much as I would like to see the cushy concubine behind bars and going into Godiva withdrawal, it wasn't possible. While the wheels never stopped turning in Connie's head, physically she was the laziest person I had ever known besides my ex.

Once Connie was worried a new employee was going to ask her to help load canned goods into her trunk for delivery to a soup kitchen. Heading her off at the pass, the Favored One ordered, "You'll have to do it. I've forgotten how."

So there was no way Connie could crouch that enormous rump behind a hibiscus bush, grab a garden gnome, spring into action, hurl herself at Louis and push him in the drink.

Donna said, "Vincent said once he was in charge, there'd be some changes at the Crisis Center."

That would scare Pete and Connie since everything was arranged exactly to their benefit, but it wasn't a mortal insult.

"What else did Louis say?"

Vincent had stared at Connie as contemptuously as when he appraised the sleazy paid tipsters at the *Intruder.* "He asked Pete if he had a succession plan in mind."

I said, "In a pig's eye."

"Yeah. Pete said a bunch of neutral, very reasonable sounding blather that wasn't really an answer. Like he usually does."

"Yeah, I'm familiar with that tactic." Pete had "the gift of grab."

"Vincent said non profits were now like the real world, where no job is secure."

Whoa! Veiled threat. I loved it. Donna was such a good friend— already she had cheered me up.

Vincent had said to Pete, "Seeing Connie here reminds me that you get what you pay for."

As Pete's face turned purple, Vincent sneered, "Judging by the freight, you must have gotten a two-for-one special."

"You think Vincent really had it in for Connie or was just yanking Pete's chain?" I asked.

"I think he was letting Pete know he was about to give a lot of money to Palm Beach Crisis Center and it wasn't going to be business as usual. They got off on the wrong foot ever since every man, woman and dog on the Island got 5 Crisis Center invitations to the function where Louis was going to be honored."

"True," I said.

"And Pete had misspelled Vincent's name on a banner for the gala," Donna continued.

Many a career in philanthropy had ended over less.

"Vincent told Pete he wanted them to inspect the party site together to see if he had any other sloppy mistakes to correct."

"Vincent said he wanted to see Pete at the Ecklunds' home?"

"Apparently, but it must have been at least a day before the Palm Beach Crisis Center gala, so there'd be enough time to correct the signage."

"That explains why Brenda Ecklund told police that Vincent seemed put out and planned to visit the party site twice in one day," I said.

Pete was like Cher—he could survive everything. He bent but never broke. He knew how to get along with his nominal overseers. He told them what they wanted to hear and then did exactly as he wanted. Pete was so practiced and so patient; Vincent would be bamboozled or get tired of trying to change things and fall into line like the rest of the Crisis Center board.

The next morning, I took my car to Manny's garage for an oil change and even though I had stacks of work waiting for me at the office, said I'd wait. When Manny went to the bay to discuss something with one of the mechanics, I pretended to go to the restroom. Then I snuck into his cubbyhole office at the back of the building. On a shelf in the wall between the restroom and his office, I spotted Manny's toolbox. I peeked in. I was afraid to touch anything. Besides Manny could be headed back at any minute. I saw the usual screws and socket wrenches and something else. Something sinister. A dirty, cracked wooden handle attached to the nastiest blade I ever saw in my life. A rusty, at least I hope it was rust, nasty-looking, ten-inch long serrated butcher knife.

I ran back into the restroom and locked the door until my breathing slowed.

I wasn't going to argue over any bill with Manny. He didn't seem to notice my restraint, as he was too busy admiring himself in his pocket mirror and fussing with his hair. I tried not to look at his dirty, callused hands as he smoothed his glossy locks. I couldn't believe I once thought he was sexy.

I had never been so happy to be back in my safe little office. In a while I'd invite Lucette for lunch so she might relax and tell me something good. I was bent over my messy desk with Peter Pignatelli entered my office. After my scare at Manny's garage, I didn't feel so hot. But my boss didn't look so hot either.

He asked, "How are the pet interviews coming along?"

"Fine," I said, trying to sound chipper. "Combined Charities was right— people are jumping all over us to get in the new magazine. They want to know if we are going go in depth on pet trust funds and whether we'll reproduce oil paintings of their favorite pet portraits."

"At $2,500 a page?" Pete lifted an eyebrow. "What do you think?"

"Give 'em anything they want."

Although, this being the Island, already there was controversy. Some people wanted *Palm Beach Society Pets* to take sides on the feral cat fight. Island residents, including Catherine Bradley, had been feeding 1,000 untamed cats for 15 years and there were now 100 cat colonies in Palm Beach. Residents complained that mangy, stinking cats were overrunning their pristine properties. Who knew if they were rabid? Or if they carried the cat scratch fever that caused blindness? To make matters worse, once the police began trapping and killing feral cats (50 in three months before the outcry stopped the program), someone scrawled "CAT KILLER" on walls and fences and tampered with the traps.

Anywhere else, a woman feeding 1,000 feral cats year after year in the middle of zillion dollar real estate would be thought of as "Crazy Cat Lady" and stopped. But not on the Island, where everyone got very emotional about wanting to appear compassionate, as long as the recipients had four legs. After much angst, the town planned to neuter the kitties and pull a Not In My Back Yard. The cats, like sewage, garbage, car lots and other unpleasant realities, would be deported to Palm Beach County. An Island resident said he'd consider paying for the land for a "cat sanctuary," complete with endless Tender Vittles and veterinary care, if it wasn't too expensive.

I would keep our nice little pet magazine out of it, or it would end up as kitty litter.

Pete said, "Hope has asked that I meet with her later today to discuss the coverage she wants in the magazine."

"Are you sure you don't want me to do that?" That was a humiliating errand for an executive director. It was kind of embarrassing how my boss was at the beck and call of these aristocrats.

He shook his head.

I continued, "I already have a stack of photos of Island pets." I handed him the thick manila envelope for his approval.

But since when did Pete tell me his schedule, even the most innocuous stuff? Never. No one on staff was supposed to know where he and Connie were at any time. Yes, we all figured the Hampton Inn and God knows where else they did their feral business, but officially we played dumb.

I inferred Pete's statement meant that Hope didn't call the meeting. He did. And what would they be meeting about?

You got me. I'd figure that out about the time someone proved there was life after death. Then Pete surprised me again.

"The National Association of Charities is having its annual convention in Beverly Hills next month. If you can think of a paper to present on fund raising and they accept it, you're in. Since I'm a top officer of NAC, they will accept it."

"Really?" I was delighted. I love to travel. Usually only Connie scored those perks and she didn't earn them via public speaking.

Pete said, "You'll have to hurry. They need a formal proposal by the end of this week."

Then Felicia paged him to put out a fire and he was gone.

Wow. I should be happy, except . . . .since when was Pete so nice?

Then my phone rang. It was from one of my Combined Charities counterparts upstairs.

"Justine, you need to alert the media about the new pet magazine," Combined Charities' flack said.

"Are you serious?" I asked. "'Alert the media?'"

"You bet I'm serious. I've been getting calls all morning. If this thing takes off we may go from quarterly to weekly!"

"Just don't make it daily. I'd have to work like a dog," I said.

Actually his judgment was spot on; the local papers would love adorable photos of furry vixens—and their pets. I went to Pete's office to retrieve my photos. He was out, but Felicia in her office next door, suggested I get my envelope from the open briefcase on Pete's desk.

Ahhhh, as I sank into my chair, I wondered which photos to select for this new Combined Charities media blitz. The one of I'd seen of Mr. Tibbs and his equally whiskered owner, Mrs. Dora Reynolds? Or how about Theodore Lenox's pet goldfish? Not exactly warm and fuzzy and besides, both owner and fish had scales. I thought I'd grab a cute one of a fresh-faced billionaire heiress equestrienne who spent hundreds of thousands of dollars of daddy's money every year so she could qualify for the Olympics.

But as I slid the photos from the envelope onto my desk, I discovered another type of amateur sportswoman. The pix were animalistic all right, but not of Palm Beach's prized pets. With my mouth gaping in disbelief, I had before me a montage of a younger Hope Louis, must have been before she was Mrs. Louis, with varied companions, and not all of them human. It was very Circus Maximus with a menage a tramp.

Knowing the way things worked at Palm Beach Crisis Center, I couldn't believe it was an accident I now had these freaky, furry photos. I was so suspicious of Felicia Harold by now, I just knew she had planted them in Pete's briefcase. Now I was sure it was Felicia who was behind the death of Vincent Louis, even if she got Manny to do her dirty work. It wasn't enough Felicia had to bump off Vincent to stop him from publishing her teenaged self at drug parties with her married boyfriend, the future Senator—now she has to humiliate Hope. Otherwise, her own collegiate peccadilloes might still see the light of day. Felicia would fight fire with fire. Pete's indiscreet photos of Hope's early career as Dr. Doolittle were easily worth ten times, say . . . .$65,000.

But where did Pete get these twisted photos? I guess he could have picked them up from someone he helped early in his career back in Reno, when he reformed gamblers in 12 steps. Maybe some of his shady friends repaid him a favor. Or, maybe Felicia's Sen. Randall had a defensive dirty tricks campaign of his own and passed them to her. He could keep his hands clean and Felicia would know how to put the kibosh on the remaining Louis.

But was Pete really going to meet with Hope Louis today to discuss stupid pet tricks? I think not. Or maybe he was, but not the kind that belong in the celebrated Society Pets magazine.

I didn't have time to show these to Donna, much as she'd like to run them on the front page of her august publication, not that the *Shiny*

Sheet's owner would ever let her. But I needed some insurance. I ran over to Sir Speedy, which as luck would have it, was having a 79-cent color copy special and ran off 8x10 glossies. I locked the copies in the trunk of my car, until I thought of a better place. Soon after, when Felicia was not in her office, I returned the "originals" to Pete's briefcase. Pete's "originals" were most likely copies of copies and he had to have a disc somewhere. Poor Hope. How long would it take her to crumple when Pete confronted her with the evidence of her nasty Noah's Ark?

Chapter 22

WATERLOO

It was time to pump Lucette about why Crisis Center cars were going at fire sale prices. I went to her cramped office. "Lucette?"

"Yeah?" She turned away from the computer. "I thought you'd be back." She wore fuzzy black leggings with a tatty, purple T-shirt that had a Dale Earnhardt logo.

"How about going for burgers at the Okeechobee Steak House? It will be my treat." Was I being too obvious? Would the cautious book keeper take the bribe?

"Let me get my cigarettes."

Palm Beach Crisis Center staff didn't go to the Okeechobee Steakhouse because it was pricey. The 1947 restaurant had a dark interior resembling those smoke-filled back rooms where politicians cut deals. Today the Steakhouse is nonsmoking, but its three rustic rooms and bar are dark as ever. Lucette and I sat in a corner booth behind a big divider.

We gave our orders to one of the skinny waitresses who apparently never ate the prime rib and sour cream chocolate cake house specialties. As Lucette and I ate our Caesar salads, I said, "I have some neighbors who want to buy a used car and I don't want to get into hot water again like I did with the Diors."

Lucette nodded and picked the anchovies off her salad. She seemed to know I wouldn't spring for an $11 lunch to help a neighbor buy a junker.

I asked, "How much is that '87 Toyota Camry we just got in?" I wanted to know if that Moonstone Mama was on to something.

"It went for $750," Lucette said as we slathered butter and chives on our baked potatoes.

"Fifteen hundred dollars you mean; I hear that's how much it's worth."

"That's how much it's worth in the Blue Book," Lucette said, "but $750 is all we got."

"In cash," I said. A different size 0 waitress with waist length hair brought our juicy grilled burgers. I smeared mine with mustard and piled on dill pickles and chopped onions. Then I scraped off the onions, since I didn't want to repel Lucette.

Lucette uncapped the mayo. "Justine, you know it's cash only for Felicia and Manny."

"True. But didn't I hear Felicia tell Manny the Toyota Camry was in good condition?"

"Yeah. I heard that too. Depending on what was wrong with it, we should have gotten more than $750," Lucette said.

"I agree, so was it in good shape?" I asked.

"Felicia told Pete that Manny found so much rust inside that it was either take the $750 or scrap it."

"So Felicia is telling Pete one thing and Manny another?" I said.

"A lot of times I've overheard the two of them dickering over price and settling it in advance between themselves. They never talk about customers."

Why would Pete, who was suspicious of everyone who worked

for him, except Connie, trust Felicia and Manny? Were they doing all the dirty work and making him lots of money, while he kept his hands clean? As soon as I washed my own hands, I'd ask.

"Excuse me, Lucette, I'll be right back." I headed to the restroom, behind the waiters' stations and in back of the bar. Then I heard a familiar voice.

"It would be unfortunate if the papers learned of your early career. I understand you were young and foolish but when this gets out, the tabloids you don't own will tear you from limb to limb. Then the *New York Times* will join the bandwagon, then the networks, then cable and you'll end up as an *E!* biography," said Pete Pignatelli.

After the photo spread I had just seen, and I do mean spread, I knew Pete's companion was the animal-loving Hope Baylor Louis. I peeked over the wall dividing what used to be the non-smoking section of the restaurant from the bar. In a tiny, dark alcove off the lounge, past salesmen yacking on cell phones and doleful men downing shots in front of CNN, Pete and Hope Louis were ensconced in a private booth. Pete leaned forward, trying to be persuasive and intimidating. Hope's back was ramrod straight and her lips curled in a glossy pink frost sneer.

My heart pounded. Instead of Pete going to Hope's mansion, as I had assumed, she probably hadn't wanted to let him in even via the servants' entrance. So they met in a working man's joint near the Palm Beach Crisis Center where her friends would never see her. The Steakhouse was between I-95 and the turnpike in wild West Palm Beach where the words "low carb" and "diet platter" were never spoken.

"Mr. Pignatelli," Hope said, in a way that conveyed more disrespect than if she had called him by his first name, "Don't you ever use that tone of voice with me again." Her voice was clipped, contemptuous and very Lady Un-Chatterly.

Hope summoned a pint-sized waitress to refill her Scotch and soda. She didn't need to impress anyone with some fancy French vintage. After all, her only witness was my boss, or so she thought. I ducked behind the wooden wall and prayed Lucette would go outside for a cigarette because I had to hear this.

Behind me a petite waitress dropped a tray of drinks which probably weighed more than she did. Pete and Hope never looked up as the socialite said, "My attorneys will hear about this pathetic attempt at extortion."

Pete muttered something pseudo soothing about Hope's playing fair and his concern about her reputation.

"Mr. Pignatelli," she said icily. "I am the one who will decide what is fair and as for my reputation, you should be the last to judge. People who live in glass houses should not throw stones."

My boss protested and his coffee cup come down a little too hard in its saucer. Clink!

Hope continued, "It's despicable the way you are attempting to take advantage of a helpless widow. Your underhanded methods won't play well on the Island."

"Mrs. Louis, please don't misunderstand me. I am only trying to protect you from the devastation the press will wreak on you should the evidence fall into the wrong hands."

He sipped his coffee and said, "I have only your best interests at heart."

Hope Louis sniffed.

Then my boss pulled his classic "I feel your pain" maneuver.

"Perhaps you would allow me to show you why I am so deeply concerned for your good name?" The nastier these two got, the more polite they sounded, very Emily Post-it-on-the-web.

I snuck another peek. The platinum blonde socialite's eyes, recently done by Flagler Drive's finest plastic surgeon, were narrowed slits, and her rhinoplastique nostrils were flared. Tremors went through her head and her lacquered dominatrix-do shifted a bit. Hope looked even more indignant than when she stood in her regal living room with her Tabloid King hubby and told me I wasn't worth $65,000.

"If I know about this . . . " Pete paused with delicate menace, "You can be sure someone else could find out. Someone unscrupulous who will take advantage of you for personal gain and if that were to happen, I could never forgive myself."

Pete reasoned, "Wouldn't it be better if you worked with me?"

Just before I could sneak another peek, the tiny brunette waitress hustled past me for the fifth time, then stopped and gave me an odd look. I shrugged as she kept standing there. "Should I bring the check?" she asked.

I shook my head because I didn't want to give myself away. The waitress frowned. I pointed to the lavish dessert cart and then gestured to where Lucette and I had been sitting two rooms away. It would cost me when Lucette got a double cheesecake with praline topping and whipped cream. But it would be worth it to hear the rest of this.

Hope slapped the table like it was Pete's face and said, "All right Pig, quit beating around the bush."

Pete smirked at Hope's choice of words. Hope was undeterred and taunted him, "All the attitude in the world isn't going to get you $10 million. Show me your money shot."

I felt grudging respect for the aristocrat from Akron. She was one tough cookie.

Pete looked taken aback at the socialite's bravado. Smoothly he extracted the manila envelope and slowly guided it across the pitted and stained table. Hope's hands shook as she slid out the photos. Being too vain to wear reading glasses, she lifted the evidence close to her unlined eyes.

The socialite studied the pictures carefully; her surgically tightened face a blank canvas. Then she snorted, sounding like the subject of the first photo. "Who's this?" she whinnied, "Mister Ed? Or Black Beauty?"

Why would the Island Icon laugh at photos of her girlish and garish gropings of great grotesque beasts, some human, some equine? Pete turned brick red and his face slowly collapsed as Hope dropped the insipid *Society Pets* photos into his lap. They were all there, the ponies with braided manes and feathered headdresses, the kittens, the puppies, the bejeweled gerbils.

"You're trying to blackmail me with hamsters? Hamsters?" Hope shook her head and took another hit of Dewar's as she examined another photo. "You're going to have to do a hell of a lot better than Mr. Tibbs. A mangy looking cat if I ever saw one. He looks rabid."

Pete was speechless.

"So much for your offer to protect me. By the time I get through with you." Hope said derisively, "you'll be lucky if you can 'protect' that two-ton tramp you call your VICE-director. For starters, someone might clue in your long suffering, dimwitted wife."

There was a snarling sound coming from the back of Pete's throat and it sounded like he was choking on his own blood. He muttered something guttural about having the real photos, before trailing off into a painful silence.

In ladylike fashion, Hope gently put her glass on the coaster, so as not to leave a water ring on the table. "Don't you ever threaten me ever again, you low-life, or I'll put your ass in a sling." She rose regally in her baby blue Chanel suit, with matching silk gardenia corsage.

"Now lets not overreact, Mrs. Louis." Pete seemed to shrink in the cracked leather booth. In her powder blue snakeskin sling-backs, Hope appeared to tower over him.

"Misunderstanding, my ass. You think Vincent and I enjoyed paying you off because you had those incriminating Vegas photos? I guess now that my husband's dead, you pulled some more pictures out of the safe and decided to go for the kill. You vulture. You make me sick."

The socialite pulled a mirror from her handbag and checked her makeup. Her hands weren't shaking anymore.

"You can forget about any more hush money, because now I know about the scam you're pulling with all the donated cars at the Crisis Center. You're ripping off your own charity. I'll throw you in jail and you won't take a shower for the next 10 years!"

Pete struggled to look calm. I couldn't figure this out. He had been blackmailing Hope all along and now she had turned the tables. But what exactly did she have on him?

Hope stated, "At the recent Support Group for the Wealthy meeting, my friend Mona Chargo confirmed what I had long suspected about your little scheme."

Pete seemed astonished; could it be he didn't know what Hope was getting at?

"When Mona found out that Palm Tran was going to cut the bus route to Palm Beach, she went to your Crisis Center to buy her upstairs maid a used car for $1,500."

"There's nothing wrong with that," Pete said.

"What's wrong is that Mona's pal who donated that car was at the same meeting and told her your thank you letter said she could only deduct $750."

Pete stared.

"I smell a rat," Hope pressed her frosty pink lips together and clicked her compact mirror shut. Her sculpted nose wrinkled. "I know you're skimming money from the Crisis Center by not giving it all the profit you make from those cars. Then you have the nerve to cheat your donors by not letting them write off the true value of their cars."

Hope had hit the bulls eye about the Crisis Center's black market and I was ashamed that she had caught on a lot faster than I did. I remembered that the $4,600 used Caddy "sold" for $2,300, as well as how Debbie Dior had been ripped off. But who would sell a car for less than it was worth?

No one.

Then why was the Palm Beach Crisis Center selling cars at half off? Because Felicia and Manny sold them at market rate, but the nonprofit agency got a fraction of proceeds since our homegrown embezzler and her Latin Lover pocketed the rest.

It was hard to believe Pete didn't know about the kickbacks. Nothing happened at the agency without his express approval and that included bathroom breaks. But the wily executive director had so many schemes going on simultaneously, ranging from harebrained to diabolical, at some point something had to slip under the radar. Plus I think Felicia was stringing him along sexually and he was blinded by her family connections.

Pete monitored his employees' Internet surfing and made them pay seven cents a copy for personal Xeroxes. Meanwhile he and the Palm Beach Crisis Center (the same thing in his eyes) were being robbed blind.

What an idiot I was. Lucette must have known that Felicia was taking kickbacks, with which she bought those gorgeous designer outfits that I drooled over each morning. Felicia had commiserated when we discussed those 50 kids we had on our waiting list because we can't afford to hire a children's therapist.

But if Lucette said anything to Pete, he would have fired her. For all we knew, Pete was sleeping with the fetish freak Felicia. He certainly gave her the eye when he thought none of us were looking.

Mrs. Harold, Felicia's own mother, had told me at the Support Group for the Wealthy that her father had cut her off. There was no maternal subsidy, as I had foolishly assumed. Felicia was on her own.

"What are you spending the kickbacks on?" Hope asked. "I've seen Connie's jewelry; it's beautiful, though a little small for my taste."

What a fiasco. The executive director could not be perceived as criminal or incompetent. Once someone as prominent as Hope Baylor Louis accused him, he was a goner. Pete had handed the ice queen of Palm Beach the perfect excuse to renege on the $10 million.

Hope hoisted her baby blue Kelly bag onto her narrow shoulder. "You stay away from me or I'll have security throw you out and put your mug shot in the *National Intruder*. And I'll send copies to your wife, sons, your entire board and to Lloyd Biggins at Combined Charities."

As Hope regally strode out of the darkened bar, Pete's last strangled words were, "Check please."

Chapter 23

SAPS AT PLAY

Tonight we Crisis Center peons had a command performance. Pete and cipher wife Susan were hosting their obligatory holiday party, known as the Staff Appreciation Party, or "SAP." It was one of those office things where no one wanted to go and there was no liquor to kill the pain. And Pete didn't want us parasites there; we infringed on his privacy, tracked dirt in and clogged the toilets.

This would be the first time the Pignatellis had hosted the SAP in their new home. Felicia, who had to know everything about everybody, said she wanted to check out how many bedrooms there were, how they were decorated and all that good stuff.

The party at Pignatelli Palace was actually to suck up to the board, who got to enjoy the munificent $400,000 home they made possible by paying the host $175,000 a year to oversee 200 employees (most part-time) on a $5 million budget. Meanwhile the Palm Beach County School District's Superintendent is paid less to manage 19,000 employees, 160,000 students on a $2 billion budget. Until this year, Pete's party had been called the "Board Appreciation Party."

"How does she do it?" Felicia whispered to me as she glanced at Connie glowering at a gallery of Pignatelli family photos. The staff shrinks were analyzing how it felt for dour Connie to gaze at pictures of her lover's three successful grown sons everywhere.

"It's not like Pete could say he was staying for the sake of the children when the last one graduated college 10 years ago," Dr. Mike said.

"And what's up with his wife and the country crock decor?" Felicia looked at the bovine memorabilia that was everywhere. There were colorful cow magnets on the fridge, a quilted cow cover for the toaster and a cozy cow calendar. Susan Pignatelli had really gotten a bum steer on how to decorate.

"If I were a Freudian, I'd wonder if this was her way of telling Pete he's full of bull," Dr. Mike said.

I shook my head. "The longer I'm at the Crisis Center, the less I understand."

And here she came, this short, cheery hostess passing Christmas cookies shaped like calves, with red sugar noses. She wore a green sweater appliqued with black and white heifers wearing droopy red Santa caps, topped with white cotton balls and little jingle bells. Oy vey. Susan had fading frizzy red hair that she pulled back in a bun and never once looked at Connie.

Pete despised her because sleeping with a woman his own age to whom he was married was not clandestine. He kept her because she made a lot of money researching microbes for Florida Atlantic University and he controlled secret bank accounts filled with her money. Susan spent a lot of time in the lab, which could explain how she stayed married to Pete.

With all the late nights Pete and Connie worked, and all the times they went to London, Athens, Honolulu, Santa Barbara and Sedona, how could Susan Pignatelli be the last to know? We Palm Beach Crisis Center staff had to hold our noses or risk losing our livelihoods because the south Florida job market was almost nonexistent. But what was Susan's excuse for not throwing the bum out?

Maybe it was the fine free furniture the couple had amassed. Pete had dibs on the home décor donated to our agency. He had taken some of the nicer couches home and stocked the office with worn, reject sofas from his old house. But I saw Pete's greed was more extensive as I recognized the dining room set, ornate china cabinet and matching console, from the cream of what had come from a Palm Beach estate a few months ago.

I scooted upstairs with Felicia and brazenly inspected Pete's home office, crammed with the latest fax, computer, printer, photo scanner, Palm Pilot—all paid for with agency funds. The nonprofit also paid for Connie's duplicate home office 10 minutes away.

Pete even got the agency to pay for his digital camera. He told the board in lieu of a raise, I would be delighted with an agency camera, which he kept while I continued to use my own 35 mm for Crisis Center business.

Connie did not want me to take her picture. She was one of those heavy women who never ate in public, although she looked like she could use some self-medicating chocolate.

But even though Pete was expanding his domestic empire, Connie Favre would never leave him. Despite her saintly preaching of poverty, modesty and service to others, (but not chastity) Pete's number two was as bought and paid for as the proverbial $2 whore. She'd stick around for more raises and perks.

Now that I had made an appearance, I could leave the Cattle Ranch and think about what to do next on the Louis case. As I walked down the street to my car, someone called my name.

"Hey, Justine!"

I turned around. There was Tom Kardos, a man I hadn't seen since I got canned by the *Shiny Sheet*. I had interviewed him about his plans to expand the Palm Beach Zoo at Dreher Park. Now THAT is a golden fundraiser. Everyone loves animals!

The *Shiny Sheet* wouldn't run Tom's photo because he didn't live in Palm Beach but I had kept it. I hadn't thought about it for a long time.

I walked over to where Tom was standing with his chocolate Labrador. "Long time, no see. I didn't know you lived here," I said. The Pignatellis lived in Blue Heron Bay, a new development starting in the 400's west of Delray Beach.

"I don't," he said. "I live in the town houses on the other side of these woods." He gestured to the nature preserve with walking path across the street from Pignatelli Palace.

"When did you move?" I said.

"A couple months ago," he said. "Meet Mohawk." Tom gestured to his pet. "What brings you here?"

Hmmmm, Tom's pup must prefer more upscale places to poop, so Tom walked Mohawk through Blue Heron Bay. Maybe I could get Mohawk to leave a souvenir on Pete's lawn.

When we last met, Tom Kardos was married but now, he wasn't wearing a ring. He was wearing cut off jean shorts and no shirt with just the right amount of hair on his chest, and legs that weren't all knobby and bumpy. There was no hair on his back, and no bald spot either. Wow, in the Game of Life, coming across such a fine masculine specimen was like hitting the lottery. Even Tom's feet, in brown leather sandals, were decent and I would never scorn those toes. (Felicia had really gotten me looking at feet too much.)

As I tagged along besides Tom and Mohawk, I explained I was in the neighborhood for Pete's Staff Appreciation Party.

Tom said, "I haven't met many of the neighbors yet. I've seen Pete and Susan around. At least your boss hosted you in his own home; ours is taking us to some vegetarian place."

"Yuck, no red meat? How can you live without meat and potatoes?

"I can't."

"I guess it's a zoological, conservation kind of thing."

Tom had adorable dark wavy hair, and there was something kind of exotic about his face, Roman maybe? His skin was darker than mine.

I studied his hands; I find myself doing that when I'm interested in a man and haven't even acknowledged it yet. His hands were nice, with sturdy, long fingers, broad palms, thick wrists. Mmmmmm.

"So what have you been doing with yourself?"

I smiled. "I'm not at the *Shiny Sheet* anymore." I tried to give the impression I had not left under a cloud and changed the subject.

"Speaking of animals, Tom, and I don't mean my ex-publisher at the *Shiny Sheet*, I'm doing a new magazine on pets."

"You should do exotic pets. Cats and dogs get a little boring. You know someone is going to complain if you don't include the family ferret."

"God, those are the ugliest little rodents. And they smell too." Well, by now, Tom should be quite convinced of my femininity. At least I had changed into a dressier blouse before I left work.

"Ferrets are not rodents," he said seriously. "They hunt rodents and are part of the mustelidae family and are related to the badger, otter, mink, weasel, wolverine and skunk."

I looked at him closely. Wow, this guy really did work at the zoo. Then he smiled in a normal guy way.

"Well, you're right Tom. At some point *Palm Beach Society Pets* is going to have to spread its wings . . . " I looked up to him to see if he got it and he did. "But for now I'm sticking to the tried and true. This magazine is getting a little complicated with all those feral cat fights. Pretty soon I'll be doing stories on the Rat Rescue League."

I waited for the rodent rundown which was not forthcoming, although with Tom's looks, I could feign interest.

"How long have you been at Palm Beach Crisis Center?" Tom asked.

"Five years."

"So you must really like it."

"Oh yes." I tried to sound positive and appreciative. When you raise money for a cause, you'd better act like you are madly in love with everything about it, or you look unprofessional and disloyal. But tonight I was worn out by keeping up the act, especially now that I was smelling rats all over Denmark—speaking of rodents.

Tom scratched Mohawk behind the ears. He seemed frisky and sweet and so did the dog. Available men are so rare that I kept expecting to see his wife or a girlfriend run out of the trees in a fury and stake her claim. Looking over my shoulder for the inevitable let down and put down made me nervous.

Tom asked, "But now you're doing what, PR?"

"Yes and I've branched out into marketing and fund raising."

"Fund raising. How's that going?"

"It's tough."

Tom looked thoughtful. "You haven't lived until you are made to pose in a pith helmet in front of Tiger Falls."

I grinned. "You showed true dedication and professionalism, Tom. Your pictures came out great."

Luckily he didn't ask what I did with the photos.

"You still live out in West Boynton?"

I was intrigued that he remembered where I lived.

"Yes, I do. The last affordable housing in South Florida."

"I come to your neck of the woods sometimes."

"You do?"

"Yeah, you're near the Wakodohatchee Wetlands. I like to go there and enjoy the peace and quiet. I also look for gators at the Loxahatchee Wildlife Refuge out by 441." He smiled. "It's nice that everything isn't all paved over . . . "

"Yet," I said. Tom was talking about the isolated manmade wetlands a couple miles west of my home. Wakodohatchee was Seminole for "created waters." The pretty park, full of birds and waterfowl, was actually a scenic way to dispose of treated wastewater.

We were back to where we had started near Pete's place.

"Is your boss all moved in?"

"Looks like it."

"I notice his garage is always packed. All kinds of furniture in there."

"Yeah." The problem with being a Pollyanna PR babe is you

won't offend anyone, but sometimes you come off as dumb. I could hardly explain why Pete had more furniture than Ethan Allen and had a big storage shed is his backyard. Knowing Pete, he was probably saving the goods for a second home up north, if he hadn't bought one already courtesy the Crisis Center and kept it a secret from Susan and our board.

Tom said, "The furniture's OK, but it's Pete's automobile collection I want. I envy his taste."

"Automobile collection?" This time when I sounded clueless it was for real.

"Yeah, I've seen all kinds of top of the line cars over there, Jaguars, BMWs, Mercedes, Lexuses . . . "

"You mean Lexi," I grinned.

"Lexi," Tom agreed. "Must get the Latin right. But the ultimate was weekend before last, when I saw the Rolls-Royce Corniche. I'd never seen one before, since there are only a few hundred in the country. It wasn't new, but it still looked great."

I was a blank. Pete always announced our plummiest donations at staff meetings and let us drool over the cars before he drove them home "for protection" and so the neighbors could see the status symbol in his driveway.

Corniches are $360,000 new, although used ones sell for around $250,000. But if a $250,000 vehicle came in I'd be writing features and shooting photos of Pete holding the car keys aloft in triumph and Connie draped over the hood. None of our car donations came anywhere close to being that valuable.

I said, "I didn't know we had gotten a Corniche. You're right, that's amazing." Tom's eyes were very dark and expressive, with thick curly lashes. His mouth was very molded, not the really thin, white lips you see on male WASP faces.

"No one is giving the zoo any Rolls-Royces. I'd dress in full safari gear with a bowie knife for that."

How about a loincloth instead? Concentrate, Justine. Focus on the Rolls. "What color was the Corniche, black?"

"No." Tom laughed that I was curious about the color instead of chatting about horsepower. Too bad I was coming off like an automotive airhead when I finally met an attractive man who might be single.

"It was silver," Tom said as I stared. "It was very dignified."

He added, "That was no ordinary car. It was a luxury vehicle—meant for Palm Beach."

Chapter 24

WOULD YOU BUY A USED CAR FROM THIS MAN?

"*I* wish I got a better look," Tom said. "Usually Pete parks his cars in the driveway, but this one he kept inside. If I hadn't been passing by when I did, and he wasn't putting away his tools, I never would have seen it."

"When was this, anyway?"

"Friday night before last. On Friday I got out early and was walking Mohawk."

I nodded like one of those bobble-headed dolls. I hadn't even asked how Tom had come up with that Last of the Mohicans name for his dog. My brain was freezing up. By now, it was getting dark and we had strolled through the preserve to Tom's neighborhood of duplexes. There were lots of bikes and kids' toys in the tiny front yards.

Tom said, "Well, I usually take Mohawk in by now."

I didn't blame him for wanting to go inside; I wasn't exactly keeping up my end of the conversation. I felt drained.

"Are you OK, Justine?"

"Yeah, I'm just a little thirsty." What was Pete doing with a silver Rolls on the day the same type of car was spotted near where Vincent Louis was killed?

"I'll get you some water, or do you want a beer?"

Liquor was the last thing I needed; I already felt foggy. "Water, please."

Tom didn't invite me inside; maybe he was as sloppy as I was? Maybe Mohawk wasn't housebroken? Maybe there was something he didn't want me to see, such as framed photos of female admirers?

Tom returned with ice water in a blue plastic cup with a Florida Panthers hockey logo.

"Tom, thanks for serving me from your priceless heirlooms!"

He grinned and I saw his straight white teeth. "I'm sorry I can't invite you in, I still have a lot of stuff in boxes, like my ferret encyclopedia."

"Tom! You're not unpacked yet and you've been here two months? You're a man after my own heart!" I wanted to know more about him but I needed to get on this Louis thing, talk with Donna, find out more about Felicia and her gangster pals. By now Felicia was probably searching the Pignatelli family attic. I should have looked in the closet for skeletons when I had the chance.

"That's not that long ago. I remember thinking the development on the other side of the woods was even fancier than I thought when I saw Pete's Rolls."

I asked, "How long was the Corniche at Pete's, Tom?"

"Not long," Tom said. "Are you sure it was donated to the Crisis Center?"

"I think so. How else would Pete have it?"

"One of his neighbors mentioned that Pete's sister and brother-in-law were in town."

"But I didn't see them just now."

"The neighbor said Pete is garaging the Rolls while they're on a three-week Caribbean cruise. He dropped them off at the port in

Miami."

"Guess I should go," I said.

Tom offered, "Should I walk you back to Pete's?"

"Thanks, but it's not far." I handed him my business card and Tom took the hint and said he would call. I turned back into the woods, wishing I had been wearing something slinkier tonight, but at least I had shaved my legs.

The next morning I wanted to find out what Felicia knew about the used Rolls that had been parked at Pete's. But she wouldn't tell me anything because she was up to her jeweled neck in car kickbacks.

By the time Felicia came to my office for our usual gossipfest, I couldn't help admiring her spectacular silk salmon palazzo pants, with matching shell and slinky long jacket with perfect coral and turquoise jewelry.

"Felicia, your shoes are exquisite," I said, appraising the turquoise beading and some new shape of heel I hadn't seen before.

How could I be worshiping blatant materialism when I knew full well how Felonious Felicia "earned" her fabulous ensembles? Had the Island corrupted me beyond repair? I told myself I complimented Felicia to lull her so I could grill her about the Rolls.

"So, Felicia, how come you didn't tell me about the best car you've gotten all year?"

Immediately, Felicia was on guard. She had been preening in my guest chair but now she sat up straight and seemed to stiffen. I hadn't let on that Hope Louis and now Pete were onto her. But a clever klepto like Felicia must have honed survival instincts. I smiled, "Felicia, Intruding Minds Want to Know."

"What car are you talking about?"

"The used silver Rolls-Royce Corniche. Or as they say in Palm Beach, 'gently owned.'"

Felicia laughed in my face and whatever had been bothering her had dissipated.

"What? Are you crazy? We've gotten a few ancient used Rolls with 100,000 plus miles and ripped leather upholstery where we're lucky to get $20,000 for them. Not that we aren't happy to take them."

Then Felicia asked me, "Where did you hear about the Rolls?"

Lets not bring Tom Kardos into the jungle, red in tooth and claw, that is fund raising in Palm Beach. Tom was a nice guy who worked with wild animals. He was safer that way.

"At SAP."

"Oh yeah, at the Cow Palace. I'm surprised Susan wasn't duded up for the rodeo with cowboy boots and a bolo tie. Do you think she was like that when Pete first married her? They were both so young."

"I have no idea. I'm sure he's changed a lot since then."

"Well his sister sure came up in the world. She's a brain surgeon who lives in a waterfront mansion in Naples. She owns the Rolls you're talking about."

"You're kidding."

"No, Dr. Mike says that's why Pete is so insecure about being in social work."

"I guess that makes sense," I said.

I dropped cars and careened into cooking. "So what did you think of those crazy cow cupcakes last night?"

"Caca," she said. "Considering Pete billed Palm Beach Crisis Center for the food, he should have gotten something nice catered in. Which reminds me, I need some coffee, see you later."

After Felicia left, I toyed with the *Society Pets* prototype. Lloyd Biggins sent me an urgent memo that I profile the Island woman who flew in a New York fashion designer to costume her dog for the annual pet parade on Worth Avenue. She swore the dog was in diamonds, but the designer let it slip they were rhinestones. "Justine, I'm counting on you to use your discretion," Biggins had written.

I was shocked. Not that a dazzling dachshund would be draped in diamonds, but that Biggins knew my name. He had never spoken to me before. This magazine must be even bigger than I thought. Biggins also ordered a feature on the pet spa Very Important Paws (VIP) which offered hot-oil fur treatments and peppermint-water massages while the VCR played Lady and the Tramp.

Right now I couldn't keep prattling over pretentious pets. I shut the door, even though it made people suspicious at the Palm Beach Crisis Center to see a closed door, and picked up the phone.

"Society."

"Donna, I need a favor."

"You got it. Have you made any progress on the Louis investigation? Jim is still on my back to cover the Orchid Society's garden party this week. Not that I mind the homemade blueberry scones and clotted cream. But I'm dying to hear if there's anything new on the case."

"My persistence is due to my extensive background as a hard hitting *Shiny Sheet* reporter," I said with fake modesty.

"I doubt it," she said. "OK Justine, what do you need?"

"I need you to call your source at the Palm Beach Police Department." "Because?"

"No reason."

"Oh, come on!" Being vague didn't wash with Donna.

"OK, I'm not really sure about this, because I'm really out on a limb here, but I think that a Rolls-Royce Corniche was the getaway car from the Louis drowning."

"You think that the same Rolls you told me about after Louis was killed was the getaway car? From a murder?" Donna's voice rose in disbelief.

"Only in Palm Beach," I said dryly.

"You got that right."

"You remember how Lee Jiminez . . . "

Donna said, "The *Palm Beach Post* saleswoman and the last person to see Vincent Louis alive . . . "

"She had seen a silver Rolls pull up, then back out of the driveway."

"Right, I remember," Donna said. "Lee was selling Vincent an ad."

I continued, "OK. Then you also remember the story that ran recently on how Island cops have installed surveillance cameras all over town to catch speeders and jay walkers?"

"And outsiders?" Donna asked.

"That too," I said.

"Yes, of course."

"What I'd like you to do is ask your police pals to go over the traffic control tapes from Friday before last and pull up the plates on any Rolls-Royce Corniches that were on the road at that time."

"Sounds simple enough, since there could only be several dozen on Ocean Avenue at the time."

"Donna, there are only a few hundred in the entire country!" I said, quoting Tom Kardos.

"What's your point?" Donna pressed. "Most of them have probably found their way here. Anyway, you're looking for a silver, older model Corniche, so that narrows it down."

"Exactly. Thanks Donna."

I doubted this would lead anywhere, but as a former reporter I didn't like to leave loose threads hanging and I felt the same way about the Louis investigation.

Pete had not come in yet. Down the hall, I could hear Felicia on the telephone, chatting up Manly Manny. I laid low in my office, writing pet profiles, returning calls and cropping legitimate farm animal photos that wouldn't frighten the horses. I began researching Nina Fletcher's soiree for her puppy, which had been one of the most talked about events of the season. Then the phone rang.

"This is Justine. How may I help you?"

"Justine, we found the car!" Donna said excitedly.

"Oh my God, that's wonderful," I said. "This is almost too easy. Something must be wrong!"

Donna paused to let the anticipation build.

"What? What?" I asked anxiously. I was squirming in my rusted out swivel chair, circa 1972.

"My friend ran the plates right away because this is the best lead he's had on the Louis case. But the tags belong to . . . drum roll please . . ."

"Donna, stop dragging this out!"

"The plates belong to, get this, not any Rolls-Royce . . . but a 1986 Toyota Tercel."

"Who switched the plates?" I asked.

"We don't know yet. The cops say the plate switcheroo means it's likely that whoever was driving the Corniche was the killer. Or at the very least 'a person of interest' in the murder of Vincent Louis."

"OK. That makes sense. So, do they know yet who owns the Tercel where plates might have come from?"

"Nope."

"Why not?"

"It was sold two, three weeks ago. The title work hasn't cleared yet and the computer system is down in Tallahassee at the moment."

"As usual."

"We've got a Toyota in limbo. We are driven." Donna cackled. "Justine, this could be the break we're looking for. Why don't you sound more excited?"

"I am," I explained, "There's just a lot of other stuff going on." I rubbed my eyes. I was worried about the fallout that was sure to come from Pete's aborted blackmail attempt on Hope. It was like waiting for the other Bruno Magli to drop.

Just then my other line started to flash. "Gotta go, Donna. Thanks mucho, muchacha. Let me know if you hear anything else."

I picked up line two. Would it be a colleague who needed emergency PR or a board member who needed a quick favor? Or would it be my canine cubic zirconium expert?

"This is Justine," I said, in a 'I'm not in the mood' voice.

"Justine? Tom."

"Tom?"

"Tom Kardos. Last night at Blue Heron Bay . . . " He sounded a little uncertain whether he still wanted to talk to me.

"Oh, TOM!" Sheesh, I sounded like a grouch. I pitched my voice so I sounded human. "Sorry about that. I'm having technical difficulties." Why was he calling and so soon? Praise be to Koalas.

Tom said, "I was wondering if you'd like me to dump some more work on you?" He sounded like he was smiling.

Time to sound cooperative, yet curious. "What kind of work, Tom?"

"If you help me at our party this February to raise money for the African savannah we're building for our wildebeest herd, I'll spot you a few drinks at the Leopard Lounge."

"And snacks, such as caviar and sour cream on little boiled potatoes garnished with fresh parsley?"

"Of course."

Mmmmm, that sounded irresistible. "I'm most intrigued," I said. "Tell me more." The Leopard Lounge was a ritzoid bar located inside the quaint Chesterfield Hotel on the Island. It was decorated in red, accented by leopard spotted carpet, velvet banquettes, waiters wearing spotted vests. It may sound lurid, but it was where Rod Stewart hit on cocktail waitresses, so you knew it was a bona fide pick up joint.

"I'm recruiting volunteers for our upcoming road rally fund raiser. It's sort of a scavenger hunt for odds and ends that have to be found on the Island. Teams in vintage automobiles will be assigned to look for rare 2-cent stamps from Morocco; lawn jockeys made of iron, not ceramic; diamond-encrusted nail files, that sort of thing."

"That sounds fun and I could use a manicure."

"Afterwards all the teams will meet at the Leopard Lounge for drinks, jazz music and collecting prizes."

"What's the dress code?" I asked, hoping he wouldn't say 'festive.' No one knew what that meant. On the other hand, 'formal,' meant I couldn't afford the right outfit.

"'Casual.' The invitations are calling for 'animal print.'"

"Count me in. How much are we looking to raise?"

"Three hundred thousand."

"That's ambitious," I said.

"We're selling raffle tickets for $100," Tom added.

"Not bad. What's the grand prize?"

"A Range Rover."

"That is so cool!" The zoo really worked that Kenyan safari theme in a way that never got old, the way the donors did. Of course I would help Tom, unless he asked me to shovel behind the elephants. It would be a chance to see him again, and in a fun setting, not some deadly dull black tie affair where a formal gown would be required. Not that he'd want to go to one.

"Tom, I'd love to help," I said. "But it could be dangerous."

He bit. "Dangerous?"

"Yeah, look what happened to Sharon Stone's husband at the Los Angeles Zoo when they got a private VIP tour. Didn't he get his big toe bitten off by a crazed iguana?"

As the Hollywood couple had entered the reptile's cage, the zookeeper told Sharon's hubby to remove his white sneakers, which to a lizard could resemble live rats. The hungry iguana then mistook his bare feet for supper. Munch! Ouch!

Tom said, "That was no iguana, Justine."

"It wasn't?"

"No, it was a Komodo dragon from Indonesia. Komodos are the world's largest lizards, ranging between five and 10 feet long. After the attack, Stone's husband got surgery for severed tendons and a crushed big toe."

"First his foot split, and then the marriage. I hope that wasn't the zoo's idea of a donor appreciation stunt," I said. "I bet you guys won't be doing that with any Islanders."

"Funny you should ask. Our African adventure fund raiser will be called, 'Night of the Iguana.'"

"Which is better than 'Day of the Ferret,'" I said. "So, tell me more about your zoo party," I added. Between ferrets and dragons I knew all I cared to about our fauna friends.

Tom explained our duties would be to drive a "sag wagon," with food, booze, snacks and sunscreen for people who might tire of the hunt. We would also be planting clues along the route for the teams. And at the champagne brunch in a private home that would be the inaugural iguana event, Tom would tend bar, I would serve trays of coconut shrimp, tempura and sushi. I could handle that.

I was delighted Tom had called and agreed to attend a committee meeting in a couple weeks and pick up my uniform, a T-shirt with a giant iguana and zoo log with VOLUNTEER emblazoned the back.

"Are you interested in seeing the printer's proof for the invitation? There's a Range Rover on the front."

"Cool."

"How about if I show it to you tonight?"

"That would be great. I'd love to see it." I was happy Tom was asking me for drinks to discuss the Night of the Iguana. Instead of dithering around and testing the waters forever, he directly asked in plain English. I was liking him more and more.

"Play your cards right, Justine and someday I may give you a ride in a Range Rover."

"A Range Rover? No one has ever donated one of those to us. Toyotas are more our speed."

"Not Rolls Royces?"

"Guess not. We're more a Dodge Dart type of agency. See you tonight."

I stopped thinking wild animals and romance and started thinking cheap cars and that's when it hit me. I had to find out where I had gone wrong on my Rolls which turned out to be a Tercel lead. Following this line of questioning was scary but how could I not? And since Donna had been sidelined, someone had to stay on the Louis case.

I had been distracted by the Island while the answer could be as close as down the hall. First, I made sure Pete was still out of the building. That wasn't easy since no one was supposed to let on where he was. Then I strolled down the corridor to Felicia's busy office.

"Hey, Felicia," I said and hoped I was being circumspect. I couldn't blurt out why I needed to know if a Toyota Tercel had come through here lately, or I could clean out my desk for good.

Felicia was on the phone with Manly Manny, her masculine and mercenary mechanic amour. She gestured for me to sit. Felicia was most animated when locking in a price. There was no mushy, lovey dovey talk here in Motor City and it was a match made in automotive heaven.

"Sorry about that," she said with a smile as she hung up. "I have to keep him in line."

"I bet you do," I said with a friendly grin, which I hoped looked genuine. It was hard trying to be casual with a known criminal who had a violent pal.

"Felicia, did we have an '86 Toyota Tercel come in recently? It was worth about $2,000?"

"Why?"

That was rude. As far as Felicia knew, I was still clueless about her klepto compulsions. I did the only thing that would work with Felicia. I dangled dollars in front of her.

"A friend of mine is in the market. His A/C is busted and he's not paying for another repair. He wants something cheap and reliable that cools down like a meat locker and he needs it fast."

She asked abruptly, "How do you know the Tercel sells for $2,000?"

This was awkward. "I looked up the Blue Book value before I got here."

"Justine, I don't tell you how to do your job, so don't tell me how to do mine."

I lost it. "Felicia, you have no problem telling Manny everything you know about agency inventory. Why not me? After all, I only work here and I've been here a hell of lot longer than you." I shouldn't have lost my temper, but her secretiveness and high handedness got to me.

She snapped, "Well, I don't know where you heard a Tercel came in, because it didn't. You are going to have to stop believing everything you hear at staff appreciation parties."

"So no one gave us a Tercel recently?" I asked. I was more

disappointed than I had a right to be. But in a way, I felt relieved.

"No. But tell your friend, the next time one comes in, I'll make him a great deal."

In spite of myself, I laughed at her Monty Hall imitation. "OK, Felicia, please let me know, but he may find something in the meantime."

"Is he interested in a comparable model?" she asked, anxiously. Felicia hated to lose out on a sale.

"I don't know. I'll find out."

With the potential of another car sale, I had soothed Felicia's ruffled feathers. At least we made plans to meet for pizza later at Zuccarelli's. So we were ostensibly still on good terms.

In the immortal words of Connie Favre, "Perception is more important than reality."

Chapter 25

WE ARE DRIVEN

*Wh*ere do I go from here? I worked at a place where my boss, a pillar of the community, was a failed blackmailer. His secretary, a cheesy CPA wannabe who should be behind bars, was dictating to me what was off limits. Both of them made Connie and even Hope Louis look good.

I still lacked what I really needed to investigate the Louis case: evidence. I stared at the Mount Trashmore on my desk—I hadn't seen my desktop in years. Some claimed it was wood, others steel, still others formica, but no one knew for sure.

But one man's junk pile was another's historical archive. There were newspapers moldering on it dating back to when Island billionaire John Kluge married a porn star and then invited Prince Charles to a benefit in Palm Beach. The royals canceled when they got wind of his wife's sordid past. It was no wonder I never threw anything out. I should be able to find the free "Cars for Sale" ads which Lee Jiminez had placed in the *Post*.

I knew the date the ads ran around Thanksgiving, a couple weeks before the murder of Vincent Louis. After pawing through the stack, I found the right era. I paged through the classified as my fingers turned black and eventually there was the freebie ad I placed myself, with the Crisis Center logo:

FOR SALE
'86 Toyota Tercel 92,000 miles gd condition
$2,000 OBO.
Call: Felicia 555-1212

I pumped my fist in victory and then fell back in my chair. Now what?

I wasn't sure I could ever lay the trap that would snare Felicia, as she was a slippery snake with a six foot tall, knife wielding associate. But as an ex-journalist, I knew I'd better line up all my facts first.

But even if I got to the bottom of all this, there was no one for me to go to. Our Crew Without a Clue was hopeless. The Rogue's Gallery at Combined Charities would sweep it under the rug and I'd be the whistleblower who got the ax. Yet if I went straight to Sgt. Hajost at the Palm Beach Police Department without going to any of my superiors first, I would be canned.

I knew Pete had not come in yet, because I couldn't hear him stirring in his lair. Pete had larceny in his soul but he was not capable of death in the deep end. Never. And why, after going to the trouble to blackmail the Louises, would he harm Vincent Louis who was going to give us $10 million? Sure the Tabloid Terror was crude and overbearing and would yank his chain, but Pete would quickly figure out a way around him.

It was impossible. Pete could not be the Silver Fox that Lee Jiminez, the *Post* advertising saleswoman, had seen enter and then back out of the Louis driveway as she drove out after Louis proofed her Sunday gala advertisement. Pete is bald and the Silver Fox in the Silver

Rolls had impressive, thick gray hair.

It was indeed possible. Pete could have popped a rug on his chrome dome and driven to the Island. After he played dirty pool with Louis, the Rolls-Royce Corniche would have rolled through Palm Beach; Pete would have gotten away before the police had set up the roadblocks. Even if he had been stopped, the Silver Fox would be above suspicion.

But Pete wouldn't put his own sister's car at risk as a getaway car. Unless Pete could arrange it somehow that the car could never be traced to him? If the tag on the Rolls belonged to the Tercel that had just been donated to the Crisis Center, it was plausible. Someone had to switch the plates from the donated Toyota Tercel with the Rolls.

As executive director, Peter Pignatelli had access to the many cars that were given to Palm Beach Crisis Center. His high class sister need never know about the little jaunt and once back home, Pete could replace the tags.

I needed to talk to Donna about this but I still couldn't bring myself to tell even my best pal who I had implicated as the driver. It still sounded way too farfetched and I wasn't ready to accuse anybody yet if ever. If my boss went down, he'd take me and maybe the whole agency with him in flames.

Just then, my party planner friend Genevieve Broussard called. "Where have you been?" she asked. "I haven't talked to you lately."

"Around. I've been writing up a storm," I said.

"I just got back from picking up my decorations at the Friends of Versailles committee meeting over high tea at the Ritz," she said. "I also picked up the latest dish."

"Tell me."

"Did you know Hope Louis met with Pete to discuss the future of the Crisis Center?"

I had to be careful here because Genevieve took Pete at face value, though of course she knew about his carnal relationship with Connie. "Yeah, he mentioned something about Hope wanting to talk with him about a new society pet magazine we have coming out."

"Palm Beach Crisis Center is publishing a magazine on society pets?" Genevieve asked. "I hadn't heard that."

"Yeah, it's a long story. Don't make me go into it." I chanted, "Who Let the Dogs Out? Woof, Woof, Woof, Woof, Woof!" I needed to release some tension and we'd see how well those air ducts worked.

Genevieve cut me off. "Keep your day job, Justine."

Little did she know how hard I was trying to do just that.

"So why do you think things went sour between Pete and Hope?" I asked.

"Hope was in a snit and told the Ladies Who Lunch . . . "

"You mean the Ladies in Waiting . . . "

"I mean the ladies who have way too much time and money on their hands, that after personally meeting with Peter Pignatelli, despite her beloved late husband's wishes, Pete had left her with no choice but to withdraw the pledge."

"That's our Hope."

Genevieve sounded shocked. "You knew about this?"

"Sort of."

"How?" Genevieve asked. "At the funeral Hope Louis was so gracious."

"Tell me about it."

"Are you telling me that Hope Baylor Louis, world renowned philanthropist, is a common deadbeat?"

"Yep."

"Listen Justine, I know Hope was mean to you, but I can't believe she'd stiff you guys."

"Believe it," I said as a pile of magazines slid off my desk.

"The new helium tank is here. I've got to inflate 36 balloons shaped like champagne glasses in 10 minutes. I'll call you later," Genevieve promised.

What should I do now?

If I tipped Sgt. Hajost to where the Toyota Tercel had been, he would soon be here at the Crisis Center, tracking who switched the plates and would trace the Rolls to Pete's sister. At some point the police would learn that Vincent had summoned Pete to the Ecklunds' home, so he could harangue him about the misspelled "Vinsent" banner.

Instead, while Vincent chatted with Lee Jiminez, Pete got to the deck first, then decked Louis once his back was turned. Pete then drove away from the murder scene in dignified fashion.

But why would Pete Pignatelli want to kill our white knight? Pete had pulled off a Palm Beach miracle. He had arranged for a charity to get more than a few crumbs from the Island smorgasbord, a triumph that would have cemented his cushy situation at the Palm Beach Crisis Center for life. Why throw it all away?

Because after the Tab Tyrant insulted Pete and his paramour Connie Favre at the Louis' house, Vincent had put Pete on notice that his luscious lifestyle was about to end. Pete is pushing 60. It's not like he could turn around and find a comparable position and accommodating mistress.

Hope and Vincent Louis despised each other. Even though Pete had nasty photos of Hope, Vincent could still stiff Pete for the $10 million, because he planned to divorce Hope and had made her sign a pre-nup. Once Vincent ditched Hope, he had nothing to fear from those Vegas pictures.

As soon as Louis paid the first installment of 50 grand to the Vincent Louis Crisis Center of Palm Beach, Pete and his consort would get the heave ho. Pete's big mistake was assuming once Louis was dead, life would go on as usual with widow Hope Louis signing the checks from afar.

Pete knew Hope wanted to clean up her Mafia Princess / yellow journalism image by being Lady Bountiful with a local charity. The Palm Beach Crisis Center was way down market and the socialite wouldn't be caught dead in our tacky offices. She'd never attend our boring board meetings filled with the wrong kind of people. She wouldn't dare issue an opinion, not with what Pete had hanging over her head. Instead Hope would be off restoring castles in France.

Hope would keep her wallet open and her mouth shut, making

her the perfect donor.

And killing Louis must have seemed like the perfect crime. He had risked everything, and as soon as Vincent Louis was dead, his widow withdrew her support and although Pete didn't know it at the time, she had the goods on him to make it stick. The Palm Beach Crisis Center director must have been beside himself.

Pete was doomed from the start, I now believed, because Louis had double crossed him. The Tabloid Trickster never intended to pay us the full $10 million.

My servant sources knew Louis was going broke. Vincent Louis was going to use the Crisis Center to stave off creditors. Once we named the agency after him at the big gala at the Ecklunds, everyone would assume he was rolling in it.

It was common knowledge that Pete always snookered his board and Louis knew that once he contributed a small amount, it would be a long time before our incompetent board asked him to pay the rest. The Crew Without a Clue wouldn't want to offend a wealthy donor, who kept promising he would come through . . . some day.

Donors pledged big bucks and then dragged their feet for years. It happened all the time. Vincent would transfer accounts and play the float until he left for Switzerland or the Caymans.

It made sense that Vincent Louis chose our declasse nonprofit because we are local and he could impress the private banks on the Island. He couldn't do that if he shored up some Chateau L'Dump for mooching Eurotrash he couldn't tap for loans.

Louis figured his trophy wife would find out the true state of affairs when she went for a divorce settlement. What Hope didn't know was that after her husband died, and she publicly reneged on the Palm Beach Crisis Center, his creditors would descend like a swarm of famished locusts on sugar cane stalks on a hot south Florida day.

And just as everything was darkest for Pete, he gambled one last time at the Okeechobee Steakhouse. That's when the Island icon smashed him like a palmetto bug under the dainty toe of her snakeskin Bottega Veneta pump.

Chapter 26

PUPPY LOVE

One of the most talked about society events this year was Nina Fletcher's fabulous birthday party for a one-year-old named Lulu, her Cavalier King Charles spaniel.

Lulu, Charlemagne, Blenheim, Bonita and Spot, along with the rest of the petite pups who arrived in Louis Vuitton carriers, sported red 101 Dalmatians party hats. While poolside they enjoyed a peanut butter-flavored doggie cake and chicken liver shaped like a tiered birthday cake served in dog dishes resembling crowns.

Their human companions dined on lobster salad and lemon sorbet at a black and white checked table set with hand painted black and white harlequin-patterned bowls resembling court jester's caps, complete with jingling bells, perched atop jet black chargers. An embroidered pillow in the shape of a bone, reading "Bone Appetit," was placed in each bowl.

Earlier Nina designed a place setting for the Norton Museum of

Fine Art exhibit called, "The Art of Beautiful Table Settings." She was also the high bidder at the museum's Designer Dog Bed silent auction, scoring a 5-foot-tall purple velvet pavilion fitted with a disco ball. The socialite also loaned a 1955 print, Joan Collins With Her Pink Poodle, to the Norton exhibit, "A Thousand Hounds: A Walk with the Dogs Through the History of Photography."

Nina gave each of her guests at Lulu's birthday a "doggie bag." They were filled with autographed copies of Nina's self-published book Lulu of Palm Beach, gourmet puppy treats, Samantha Kluge-designed diamond dog tags, 18-carat Love Puppy enameled charms with diamond collars that matched the guests' breeds, canine sunglasses called "Doggles," dog umbrellas known as "PetBrellas," leather leashes in rainbow colors, puppy squeak toys and a DVD recording the event.

Man, that is one lucky dog. I got up and stretched my arms over my head. One story down, eight to go.

It was late afternoon and I had to grind out more pet party stories. But Nina Fletcher, that canine-crazed old bag, I mean philanthropist, would be a hard act to follow.

Felicia strutted in my office on magenta Jimmy Choos, with little tinkling gold Roman coins. She admired the photos of Lulu.

"That puppy is adorable. Is that Nina's dog, Lulu?"

I grunted.

"She looks blissful."

"She ought to be. She was the guest of honor at one of the Island's best parties." I said. "My wedding should be so fancy. Not that my family needs to be encouraged with any 'bon appetit' signs."

"I'm glad you're writing about Nina's luncheon. Mom said it was one of the best ones all Season and I wish I had been invited." Felicia looked down. "Lulu's birthday party was the real Palm Beach."

"The real Palm Beach?"

"Yes. It was a private party, not one of those corporate sponsorship things."

"You mean Nina didn't get Alpo to chip in to entertain her friends?" I asked. "Why not?"

"Don't get me wrong. Corporations give the best door prizes, but which has more cachet?" Felicia asked. "A product pitch, or an Island hostess entertaining a select few in her own home?"

"I see what you mean."

Felicia pointed to my headline: Palm Beach Goes to the Dogs.

"You're not really going to say that."

"No. I was just fooling around."

"Then what are you going to write?" she asked.

"How about, 'Puppy's Party a Howling Success.'"

"I can do better. How about, 'I Love Lulu!'"

"Doggone, Felicia, that's perfect," I said. "Thanks."

She grinned.

How could Felicia be so fond of puppies and parties and still be an accessory to a murder? Or would she murder only for accessories?

Felicia said, "Speaking of private parties, I can't do pizza tomorrow. You want to grab a drink tonight instead?"

"I can't. I'm meeting a friend after work for Happy Hour," I answered.

I had promised to meet Tom Kardos at City Place, the downtown outdoor shopping plaza. Tom and I were meeting at Brewzzi's, where I'd drink Tropical Madness, their lime-flavored beer and check out his "Night of the Iguana" invitation.

After I left work I planned to go to the Palm Beach Mall and buy a slinky black dress to wear with my little zebra print bag. I would be both trendy and animalistic, which would be perfect for a date with a fund raising zoologist. I couldn't afford to buy the dress at the City Place boutiques and not too many other people could either. This was why the expensive shops were closing and the city was trying to land a Target.

"Another time, then," Felicia said. Then she got to the real reason she had stopped by.

"Justine, I found another car for your friend. It's not a Toyota, but it's comparable. An '82 Hyundai."

That hustling hussy never stopped. I said, "That's great, Felicia. I'll let him know."

"Does he have cash?"

"I don't know."

"Well, tell him he needs to decide fast, because these Hyundais always go like hot cakes," she said. Felicia swathed her body in pastel silk, but her soul screamed red and yellow plaid sports jacket.

"I will."

"Do you want me to call him?"

Pushy, pushy.

"That's OK, Felicia, I'll tell him later."

Her eyes glittered. She didn't want to lose the sale. "He isn't going to any of those used car lots, is he? Those people will rip him off. They're no good. Believe me, I know."

"He's not. I told him to go to you."

"Good," Felicia said. "Tell him not to wait too long or someone else will beat him to it."

"Got it."

She left with a friendly wave that jingled the dangling golden coins on her new bracelet.

Felicia didn't know it yet, but she was about to have a personal crisis at the Palm Beach Crisis Center now that Pete was on to her. He'd wait a while and then discreetly fire her. Drowning was out since there was no agency swimming pool. The Crew Without A Clue would never hear about it, just as they would never hear about the car kickbacks.

Pete would turn on me like a rabid dog if I ever spoke up about the Louis investigation. How could I live on $250 a week in unemployment compensation? That's if I could get it after Pete blackballed me on the Island with some trumped up charges.

And why was Pete being so nice to me all of a sudden, offering to take me to lala land? He always threw the perks to Connie and lately to Felicia while the rest of the harem, which didn't put out, went without.

I had wanted to look sleek for my date with Tom tonight but I was worked up thinking about the murky Louis case. I got my hairbrush and hot coral lipstick so I could freshen up.

Just then the buzzer on my phone lit up.

I picked up the receiver. "Yes?" I said as pleasantly as I could.

"May I see you in my office, please?" my boss asked politely.

I was filled with dread. I'd rather do my chatting with cold blooded killers in a well-lit public facility.

"Sure," I chirped. "Just give me a second."

Whenever Pete had a project at 5:00 p.m., it could never be wrapped up in a less than a few hours. I called Tom.

"What's the matter?" he asked, when I postponed.

"Nothing," I said. "My boss just told me I have to work late tonight."

Tom said, "I can wait. I've got plenty to do here."

"No, please, I'd rather we go out tomorrow night, if that's good for you."

"OK, if that's the way you want it . . . " he sounded annoyed. "I'll bring the invitation tomorrow. Same time, same place?"

"Sure," I agreed, but Tom didn't sound as happy as he had before. Had I blown it with him before we even got started? But I needed to hang on to my job as long as I could.

I took my pen and notepad and walked what felt like the Last Mile to my boss's corner suite. I was relieved to see that Felicia was still in her office next to Pete's, chatting over the phone with Mendacious Manny.

Felicia owed Pete big time for taking a chance on her and she'd repaid him by robbing him and jeopardizing his position with the agency and the community. With loyalty like that, he could skip buying her a gift for Secretary's Day. No more Hallmark cards for you, honey.

After Hope had practically spit on Pete today, he must be

distraught. And even $100,000-a-year Connie Favre had failed to sniff out Felicia and her scheme. A guy as let down as Pete may feel he deserves something new.

As soon as I walked in he said, "Shut the door."

I closed the door and hovered with my hand on the knob. Pete looked puzzled that I didn't pull up a chair and plop down as usual.

"Justine, please sit down."

I perched on the edge of the guest chair nearest to the door. I snapped opened my notepad in a businesslike Girl Friday manner.

Pete stared at me so intently I got the creeps. Under the harsh fluorescent lighting that magnified the liver spots on Pete's head, the vibes grew stronger. As Pete gazed at me with a fixed smile, I got the message. He thought some sexual healing was in order. Why couldn't he just go home like other men and watch *Law & Order*?

I jiggled my pen like it was out of ink so he wouldn't see my hands shaking.

"Pete, if this is about Lulu Fletcher, I mean Nina, the story is done," I said in a rush. "However, I'm still running down the rhinestone angle on the Worth Avenue pet parade because people are stonewalling on the carat count. I need more time."

"Who is Lulu Fletcher?"

"She's the Palm Beach puppy who was guest of honor at a big birthday bash. She's going to be the centerfold."

Pete nodded. "Justine, how long have you been working here?"

"Five years." But with *Society Pets* it seemed like 10. With the Louis investigation, it felt more like 20.

"I know we haven't been able to pay you much—no one in this shop makes anything—but I just wanted to let you know how much Palm Beach Crisis Center in general and I in particular, appreciate your outstanding work."

He added, "Your willingness to take on the celebrity pet project speaks volumes."

He relaxed and leaned back like he was ready for a cigarette. This was even stranger than the west coast junket Pete had offered me earlier.

Pete said, "I look forward to seeing your new speech."

My speech? Oh yeah, the fund raising seminar I was supposed to give in L. A. Naturally, with all the snooping I'd been doing, lurking behind waitresses in a steakhouse stake out, I hadn't written one word.

"I look forward to seeing it myself," I laughed, trying to sound natural. "I haven't started it yet because of my pet project."

"Well, you'll have time to polish your presentation on the plane, where I've booked us both seats in first class." He looked at me expectantly. I was supposed to thank him lavishly for this signal honor.

"Why, thank you," I said stiffly. "That's very nice."

"Connie and I have earned many frequent flyer miles while on agency business and since Connie won't be traveling with us, she has kindly offered to give you her seat."

Oh my God, Pete must be punishing his former favorite by ordering her to stay home. Connie would be coming after me with a serrated butcher knife. The spot between my shoulder blades itched.

"Oh, that's so sweet of her," I said.

"It's a long flight," Pete said. "We'll both be comfortable and it will give us a chance to focus on your career." His broad smile was scarier than his usual glower.

"Well, that's just great. I really appreciate your looking out for me," I said like a perky Donna Reed with apple cheeks and a ruffled red checked gingham apron. "I should get started on that speech."

Maybe I would have time to reach Tom at the zoo and we could still get together tonight.

"It's closing time, Justine. The speech can wait until tomorrow," Pete said. "Are there any concerns you want to discuss? You can confide in me."

"Concerns?" Yeah, self preservation was the primary one. I wondered how soon would it be before Connie lied about me so I'd get the ax.

"Why, no. I don't have any concerns." I tried to look carefree.

"I'll have Felicia . . . " his voice grated alarmingly on her name;

"make all the transportation arrangements. I'll send a limo to your home to take you to the airport."

Pete waited for more expressions of undying gratitude.

"Thanks Pete, I am not worthy." I gave a half salute and rose from the chair. "I guess I better go now."

He looked disappointed. Over the years, I had caught the seductive undercurrents, with Pete sitting next to me at meetings when Connie wasn't around, trying to catch my eye by gazing into the side of my face until I looked at him. He dropped hints about wanting to get to know me better, which I always ignored. Pete never crossed the line into an actual proposition because I played dumb and because he knew the staff was on to him and Connie. He was hyper aware of the sexual harassment laws.

As I pushed my chair away, Pete stood and picked up his briefcase, with God knows what peep shows inside. "Justine, it's been a long, hard day," he smiled.

"You're telling me."

"I think the two of us should reward ourselves with a nice dinner and maybe even a few well deserved drinks," he said, with a scary twinkle in his gimlet eye. "Have you ever been to the Sailfish Club?"

"No."

"Susan and I are members. Shall we go there? After that eulogy you wrote, you deserve a special treat."

"You must be kidding," I blurted.

That was not diplomatic and I started to sweat. How could I get out of this situation?

Pete pretended not to realize I had just insulted him. "Your Vincent Louis eulogy was very well received."

"That's not what I meant," I said.

"Oh, you don't like the Sailfish Club? They have the best fresh seafood in the state, the finest collection of single malt liquors and the waterfront view is unparalleled."

Maltz, schmaltz. "I'm sure the Sailfish Club is fine," I said, "But I don't think we should go there."

"Then where should we go?"

"Nowhere. You're a married man." How obvious did I have to be?

He laughed, oh so suave, oh so Cary Grant. "Justine, I thought you were more sophisticated than that."

"No, actually I'm not," I said eagerly. "I'm really unsophisticated considering I work on the Island."

"Justine," he said.

"Yes?"

"We are more than friends."

"No, we're not."

"We could be."

"Pete," I pleaded, "Please stop putting me in this awkward position."

"There won't be anything awkward about our positions."

"Stop it!"

His face turned brick red, since he'd seen my refusal as the second attack on his manhood today. But Pete must have been desperate to sleep with someone outside his roster of Felicia, Connie and Susan. I didn't blame him.

"Justine, I find it hard to accept that a hard working young lady like yourself would not want to enjoy an elegant business dinner that would give us both a great deal of pleasure."

"I'm sorry," I said.

"You don't have to worry that I'm your superior. After all these years, let's not stand on ceremony."

Pete put the "sin" in sincerity.

"I can't." Farewell livelihood, but I had to draw the line somewhere.

"Is it because I'm a little older than you?" he wheedled.

(You mean the mere 30 years between us?) "No, that's not it."

"Then why are you being so timid?" he asked. "Do I have to gentle you into this?" He came around the desk to seal the deal. I backed up against the wall. How could get I get him to stop?

He put both palms on the wall on either side of my face. He was going in for the kill . . . er, the kiss.

Before he could touch me, I blurted, "I saw the photos, Pete."

His heavy lidded expression didn't change. "What photos?"

"Your three-ring circus shots of Hope Louis and her mascots. They're disgusting. So are you."

The air in the room went still. Was he going to slap me? I smelled stale coffee on his breath and his snaggle teeth were yellow. He looked me in the eye.

"You must be mistaken," he said. It was an order.

"Get away from me," I said.

Pete returned to his desk and I sagged against the wall with relief. He reached into the same briefcase that a few hours earlier held the Vegas shots and pulled out a gun.

I couldn't believe it. This was a man who did not take rejection well.

"It was an accident," I babbled. "I didn't switch the photos on purpose."

My ex-boss ignored me and I grew more flustered. "That's not a real gun, is it?" I asked. The gun Pete aimed at me was strange and old fashioned looking. He gestured for me to open the door and then I could see the entire office was empty and dark. Everyone had left, including Felicia. The girl had impeccable timing.

"Where did you get that thing?" I asked inanely.

"A donor was kind enough to give the agency his entire gun collection," Pete said as he loaded his firearm. "And his bullets."

He walked up close behind me and jammed the barrel in my back. "Start walking."

Chapter 27

ALLIGATOR ALLEY

We walked through the building and didn't see anyone else. There was no therapist was working late, no night custodian. While the Combined Charities lobby was lit like the Sahara at high noon, our entryway resembled the dark side of the moon. Except for our two cars, the parking lot was empty.

Pete still had his gun at the small of my back and his other hand gripped my shoulder. He walked me towards his car. I knew once I got in, it was all over. I stumbled. Pete shoved me and said, "Move it."

Did something flicker in the shadows by the bushes next to the building? Out of the corner of my eye I thought I saw a man crouched in the bushes. Or was I seeing things?

It was Tom.

What was he doing here? He thought I had blown him off and I thought he had written me off. While Pete popped the locks on his car I snuck a glance at Tom and saw the shocked look on his face. He

171

couldn't see the gun pressed into my back, but he saw how close Pete and I stood in the dark, which gave the impression we were headed to the No Tell Motel.

Pete strengthened his pincer grip on my shoulder and I had to decide if I should fight. If I resisted, Pete might lose what was left of his composure and do away with me right here and Tom could get shot too.

If I appeared to cooperate, there was a chance Pete would calm down and I could talk some sense into him. I looked around. Tom was gone.

Pete wasn't going to shoot me in his car; it would be too messy with all kinds of DNA left behind. I'd make sure to touch as many surfaces as I could to leave my fingerprints. But what if he wiped them down . . . after?

Whatever Pete had in mind, it wasn't a fish dish with the elite. Instead Pete headed west to the turnpike, then south, exiting near my home in west Boynton Beach. He turned south on Jog Road, which was dark and lonely this time of night.

Maybe I could still jolly him out of it.

"OK Pete, it was a nice drive, but the delis are on Hagen Ranch Road." Pete didn't answer but his jaw twitched.

He turned left into a dark, narrow parking lot. Pete got out of the car to remove a barrier in front of the entrance to the closed Wakodahatchee Wetlands. This was my chance. I tried to make a break for it and I wrenched the door handle. But Pete had child proofed the locks and I couldn't get out on my side. I scooted to the driver's side but Pete blocked me. With a nasty, knowing smile, he pulled me out of the car.

"Pete, look . . . " I said, trying to placate him.

"Shut up."

I had been here before. Wakodahatchee was a glorified swamp. I heard strange birds cry and their prehistoric laments echoed across the lake. The moon was low in the sky, huge and golden and remote. The suburbs seemed very far away.

Vincent Louis had died in a manmade watery grave and it looked like Pete planned the same fate for me.

The last time I had been here during the day I had seen vultures. Now I heard an owl and a loon, besides the one shoving me along the three-quarter-mile boardwalk over the Wakodahatchee ponds. We passed a sign that warned about bobcats.

"DANGER: Bobcats have been on the prowl. Visitors are strongly advised to not proceed beyond this point."

We kept going and I dragged my feet. Who was more dangerous: the wild animals in the woods, or the wild animal with the gun?

"Pete, I know you didn't mean to kill Vincent Louis."

"Of course I did."

"Oh." I didn't have an answer for that.

"Justine?"

"What?"

"Can you swim?"

"Yes, I can."

"Too bad. I'll have to shoot you first."

I gulped.

" . . . and the alligators can finish you off."

We were silent.

Could I have screwed up any worse when I assumed it was Felicia who was behind the murder of the Tabloid King? I had wasted all that time pursuing a petty thief with a sordid past when I should have been targeting my own boss. And now it was too late.

I could barely move my legs, I was so scared. I found myself wishing I hadn't pissed off my potential boyfriend on what was turning out to be the last night of my life. Tom would believe I had been sleeping with my boss and was probably home by now, feeding Mohawk. I groaned.

Then the whacko from Wakodohatchee decided to reveal his enlightened side. "Justine, compassion is crucial at Palm Beach Crisis Center. After all I've been through, how can I free you when you don't have the slightest hint of sympathy for me? Your coldness disturbs me."

He was disturbed all right. We both knew once he got me alone deep in the swamp, I was bobcat bait. We were far away from the road and civilization. The mosquitoes swarmed in the humid night and we passed more warning signs.

"I'm sorry if I behaved badly, Pete."

"IF?" he sounded wounded.

"OK. I'm very sorry THAT I wasn't nice to you earlier when you uh, befriended me."

"Well, that's better than no apology at all," Pete said.

"How can I understand what you are dealing with, Pete, when I don't know what really happened at the Ecklunds?" I asked.

He shook his head.

"I'm serious. Intruding Minds Want to Know. You can tell me."

He faced me and for the first time lowered his weapon. "I did the world a favor by getting rid of that bastard. Who will miss the man who printed the *Intruder*?"

"No one."

"His own wife was thrilled to see him go."

"True."

"It's not like I knew what was going to happen when Louis ordered me to the Ecklund's pool to kiss his ass one more time before his big party." Bullshit. Pete had already disguised himself with the toupee and had switched the plates from the donated Toyota onto the silver Rolls.

"That is such a relief to hear, Pete. I knew it had to be an accident. You would never be premeditated." I tried to sound warm and encouraging but my voice shook.

"Of course not. I am fully self actualized."

Pete slings around the New Age phrases to motivate staff to work like dogs. But I never thought he really believed in that self esteem crap. I guess there were a lot of things about the Crisis Center I hadn't known, until it was too late.

"Even Connie doesn't know this, Justine," Pete said.

"Thank you for confiding in me," I said. "How about Susan?"

"Especially not her," he said with contempt and irritatedly swatted a buzzing mosquito.

"The bigger they are, the harder they fall," Pete sneered. "Louis never knew what hit him."

"Louis couldn't swim," I said. "You didn't even need to hit him with anything, just a good shove would have done the trick."

"Too bad I didn't know that. It would have saved me a lot of trouble." He chuckled.

He grinned. "You were interviewed by the cops, weren't you?"

"Yeah."

"I wasn't, even though Hope immediately suspected me," Pete said.

"Why not?"

"Because I had been blackmailing the two of them for years with another set of Vegas photos. She wasn't about to go to the police." He snorted.

"But Hope didn't know for sure you had killed him."

"No, but she had the last laugh when she withdrew her husband's $10 million pledge. It was indecent; she couldn't even wait until he was in his grave."

I asked, "Pete, couldn't the two of you have compromised somehow?"

"Why should I let her off the hook after all I've been through for this agency?"

Since I didn't trust myself to speak, I made a sound to show I was impressed with his many accomplishments.

Pete asked, "Have you ever read James Jones?"

Where did that come from? "Yeah, *From Here to Eternity*."

"In one of his other books he describes 'the untold buckets of shit' he had to eat to advance in the military."

I nodded.

Pete added, "That's nothing compared with the charity racket."

"Really?"

"Do you know how many hours I've put in to build Palm Beach Crisis Center from a little jerkwater two-man office into the premier agency it is today? My blood, my sweat, my tears."

Again I nodded.

Pete withdrew a handkerchief from his pocket and wiped his forehead. "Can you imagine what it's like to report to that arrogant bastard Biggins and his Combined Charities goons?"

"They're thugs," I agreed.

"You'd have bleeding ulcers too if you had to kowtow to half the Island to get them to throw a few scraps from the table," Pete said.

"No argument there."

"Over 1,000 clients depend on me," Pete said, "ME."

"Where did Hope fit into all this?" I asked.

"She was supposed to disappear while I ran the place."

"What about her moving to France to be a Marquessa?"

"It's possible," Pete said. "She'd do that just to avoid me. She's really afraid of me because she knows I have the whip hand."

"Not anymore you don't."

Ouch. I shouldn't have said that. Satan looked at me out of the side of his eyes and something evil glinted. "I'm in control here."

I had hoped if I got Pete talking, he'd calm down, realize there was nothing to be gained from getting rid of me and cut me loose. But he was boasting about his conquest of the Tabloid King because dead women don't talk.

"Listen Pete, if anything happens to me . . . "

"Justine!" Pete sounded shocked at my poor taste.

"Sorry Pete, I didn't mean to be rude." God, that man was exquisitely sensitive—to his own feelings.

I began, "But just in case you're planning anything, I have copies of all Hope's Greatest Show on Earth photos tucked away." Meaning my little Sir Speedys were still in the trunk of my locked car in the Palm Beach Crisis Center parking lot.

Pete gestured with his gun. "Justine, I'm not going to shoot you, not if you don't force me. The decision is up to you."

We were at some kind of a standoff. He had already killed once—did he need to get up the nerve to murder again? What was he waiting for? Maybe he was more nervous than I thought and maybe I still had a chance.

I played for time. "I'm not the only one who knows about Felicia and Manny. The Support Group for the Wealthy knows."

"So what?"

"You can't kill all of us."

Pete mulled this for a moment. "It doesn't matter."

He lifted the gun. "Those biddies can be written off as Island gossips. They aren't going to say anything about being ripped off, because they don't want to go public and embarrass themselves. You're another story." He swatted at another mosquito, smearing blood along his turkey neck.

I heard something in the woods. Bobcats? Below the boardwalk I heard what could only be alligators grunting and swishing in the dark, the water lapping amidst lily pads and twisting snakes. I knew from past excursions the water beneath was shallow, bottle green and smelled rotten. I heard a strange caw from a distant bird. It was definitely a loon.

Pete seemed to deflate. Maybe the past few weeks had caught up with him? Maybe I'd be OK after all? I started to edge away. He roughly grabbed my arm and whipped me over to the rail above the murky lake. He jerked my arm one more time, just for emphasis.

He put the gun to side of my head.

"Jump."

"NO!"

I shoved my elbow into his pudgy waist and ran. I couldn't believe I had the nerve, but it was either me or him. I leaped off the boardwalk onto the soft, mucky ground at the shore.

For an older guy, he moved fast. It must have been all those workouts at the gym. And he was desperate to get rid of me. He clawed the back of my neck and force marched me from the dirt path into the sludge, and into the water. At first it was so shallow that I could stand.

But as he stood above me with the gun, I began sinking into the slimy lake bottom. The more I pumped my feet to stay afloat, the more stuck I got. And my thrashing was announcing to every alligator in the swamp, "Suppertime!"

My hand closed around a rock from the lake bottom. I threw it at Pete and missed. It landed with a large splash.

"Justine, don't move!"

I froze. That wasn't from Pete. I heard multiple splashes at the opposite end of the lake. Someone was throwing big rocks into the other end of the swamp to draw the gators. Pete ran towards the stranger. I dog paddled, then half staggered, half climbed out of the swamp water. I lost both shoes in the sucking muck.

Pete hesitated when he heard me heave myself out. For a split second, he didn't know who to go after first, me or the rock thrower. But Pete had a job to finish. He came for me.

I couldn't move without shoes. Pete tackled me and knocked my breath out as we landed in the mud and slid. He pinned me with his arm across my throat. I shouted when he flopped me over so I was lying with my face pressed into the ground. He grabbed my hair and started dragging me back to the swamp head first like I was a cave woman.

He panted in my ear, "Since you won't drown, I'll beat you bloody, then the gators will smell you and finish you off. The bobcats can feast on anything that's left."

I screwed my eyes and mouth shut as he held my face down in the pond. The water rushed into my ears and I tasted brackish liquid. I held my breath as my heart pounded and my temples went black.

Suddenly I felt a rush of air. I was free. I sat up, choked and rubbed water from my eyes. Pete hadn't let me go. A man had hurled himself on Pete who had rolled off me and thudded to the ground. They grappled for the gun when Tom slipped and fell. Before he could get up, Pete ran for the lot and drove off with the tires squealing.

Tom returned to me as I was on all fours gagging from the scum that plugged my nose and mouth and even my ears. My hair was slick with mud. I wondered if any snakes or tadpoles had crawled in anywhere.

"Justine, are you OK?" Tom asked. He wiped mud from the corner of my lips.

"Yeah, I think so."

"You're not hurt anywhere?" he said, putting his hand gently under my grimy chin and looking at one side of my face and neck and then the other.

"No, I'm fine. How did you know I was here?" I asked.

"I've been following you since I saw Pignatelli holding you in the Crisis Center parking lot."

"We weren't cuddling, for God's sake. How disgusting. He was kidnapping me," I stated the obvious. I should thank Tom for rescuing me, but the thought of Pete pawing me made me wretch more than the filthy water I had almost swallowed. I wonder what kind of bacterium and amoebae lived in these sewage treated waters? I hoped I didn't get infected.

In the distance we heard sirens.

Tom was being reasonable. "I stopped by your office because I was mad at how quickly you blew me off with some lame excuse about working late for the boss. Then I saw the two of you together."

I spat on the ground to get rid of any one-celled creatures that might still be floating in my saliva, not from what Tom had said. I wiped my mouth.

"Where were you parked?" I asked. "I didn't see your car."

"I didn't realize your building had two entrances. I parked on the side that was lit. But when I didn't see signs for your agency, I walked around to the other side of the building," he said.

"Then I saw the look on your face when Pignatelli forced you into his car," Tom said. "Then I followed you . . . "

"I'm so glad you did, Tom. Thank you."

"I knew you lived in west Boynton and it appeared you and Pete were going home. I didn't know what the hell was going on. "

The sirens were much closer. I was giddy with relief and got to my knees as rivulets of water rushed down my pant legs. My clothes squished. Tom put his hands under my armpits and heaved me up.

"I knew it wasn't your idea to come here when Pignatelli turned into the park."

"Why not?"

"Justine, you don't know a ferret from a rat. So what would you be doing on a nature trail after dark?"

"True."

"That's when I called the cops from my cell to report an abduction," Tom said. "When you were clomping on the boardwalk, I trailed you in the dirt. Pignatelli was such a blowhard, and you were trying to make so much noise to drag things out, neither of you heard me."

By then we could see flashing blue lights amidst the trees and hear a radio squawking. We hobbled into the parking lot to see four Palm Beach County sheriffs surrounding Pete. He was facing a squad car as they cuffed his hands behind his back. I was looking for his gun when Pete made his last executive decision.

"You are not taking me to jail!" His eyes darted, but his face was fierce.

One burly cop laughed. Another rolled his eyes. The third said sharply, "Sir, please get into the car."

"I am not going to jail," Pete declared.

"Sir, into the car." The cop sounded even more definite and put his hand atop Pete's head to guide him into the back seat, which had been lined with a plastic sheet.

Pete shook him off.

"I'm going to kill myself!" he said.

The cops looked at each other. As soon as a perpetrator claimed he was suicidal, jail was out of the question.

"Take me to 45th Street," Pete shouted. "I demand to be committed!"

Chapter 28

PALM BEACH JU$TICE

CRISIS CENTER TO HONOR HOPE LOUIS
By Donna Shaughnessy, *Palm Beach Daily News*

> The Hope Louis Crisis Center of Palm Beach will
> honor philanthropist Hope Louis at a cocktail
> reception at Café L'Europe on Friday, December 1, at
> 6:30 p.m. The non-profit, social service agency which
> serves hundreds of vulnerable local families, changed
> its name when the heir to the *National Intruder* fortune
> said she might consider restoring her late husband's
> pledge of $10 million.

> This occasion gives us the opportunity to honor one of
> the Island's biggest benefactors," said Franklin S.
> Harold, the new president of the Crisis Center. "We

also plan to make a few surprise announcements."

The Crisis Center has undergone a management shakeup in recent months, with the departure and subsequent incarceration of executive director Peter Pignatelli, convicted in the death of publishing magnate Vincent Louis. The agency survived a steep drop-off in donations through income derived from sales of pages in the magazine *Palm Beach Society Pets*, as well as the expansion of its Support Groups for the Wealthy franchise. The Crisis Center is hosting the upcoming Louis gala to announce it is re-entering the charity circuit just in time for Season.

Harold explained, "When Willie Sutton was asked why he robbed banks, he answered, 'That's where the money is.'"

It's the same with poor charities which need to raise funds," he added. "Only the flexible and entrepreneurial will survive. And if that means moving social services to Palm Beach, then so be it. We'll do whatever it takes to subsidize services for the less fortunate elsewhere."

The Crisis Center has chosen the theme "Vive la France," to honor Hope Louis's enduring love for her adopted country and her goal to restore the royal grandeur of its national monuments.

To RSVP call: Felicia Harold at the Hope Louis Crisis Center of Palm Beach, 555-1234.

"Garcon, more vino s'vouz plez," I muttered under my breath at Café L'Europe, home to the snootiest waiters this side of the Pyrenees. I needed a stiff one after running around all day getting everything ready for tonight's Hope Louis fete. The Crew Without a Clue was so excited when Hope dropped a hint she was willing to consider restoring Vincent Louis' $10 million pledge, it couldn't move fast enough to flatter her. It didn't occur to them if Hope really had the money she'd be in Paris already.

"I still can't believe they named the agency after Hope when she has never given more than a few grand a year," Donna said at the Crisis Center tribute. "This whole sorry spectacle reminds me of the story I did about the Caldwell Theatre in Boca Raton."

"What story was that?" I asked.

"Mr. Caldwell was the founder of Rubbermaid and had a home in Boca. He wished the theater well a few times and the theater put his name on their wall."

"Why'd they do that?"

"They probably assumed it would obligate him to donating big bucks. But Caldwell never gave the Caldwell Theater a dime," Donna said.

"That makes the Crew look politically astute," I said. "I didn't think that was possible."

"Then the theater's gesture backfired when potential donors saw Caldwell's name on the marquee and assumed it didn't need money."

"Oy vey, that does sound like our Crisis Center," I said.

"'The Hope Louis Crisis Center,'" you mean," Donna said.

"Don't rub it in," I said and unsuccessfully tried to signal a waiter. A Gallic gargoyle with thick gray hair and eyebrows knit ferociously in his hawk face, sneered at me. He had seen me hours earlier getting ready, so he knew I was a peon of Palm Beach.

Then he recognized Donna and a light flashed in his beetle eyes. He whispered to the maitre d' and suddenly we were surrounded by officious waiters in tuxes and faux accents, offering Bordeaux, along with trays of canapes and puff pastries. Yum, I could see why the restaurant won south Florida's cherished Golden Spoon award for haute cuisine, but not necessarily for service.

At least I would look good at this travesty. I had on a Tuleh party dress, which was long, pink and flirty with a ruffled neckline. It combined Palm Beach's two biggest designer musts, coral and floral. Of course, my dress wasn't actually "new." I had snagged it at a consignment shop in an alleyway, courtyard that is, a few blocks east of the *Shiny Sheet*. Let's hope that Hope's estranged daughter, who wouldn't be caught dead honoring her mom, had never worn this outfit, or I would hear about it tonight on the public address system.

Hope had agreed to be honored on two conditions: that the Crisis Center would host the party here at her favorite Island restaurant and that it would donate $10,000 to her personal foundation, Save the Castles. Hope had probably pocketed the check.

Party planner Genevieve Broussard had decorated our private room with Eiffel Tower replicas, the French tri-color and movie posters advertising French cinema.

"I see Hope didn't move to France as planned," Genevieve said.

Donna said, "No, but her latest French restoration project is coming along splendidly."

Hope was keeping company with a French count, who was a real aristocrat, unlike the fakes who swarmed the Island.

"Let's hope he's not like Count Jean de la Moussaye," Genevieve said, referring to the last French aristocrat to excite Palm Beach. The sometime boyfriend of Roxanne Pulitzer, de la Moussaye's title was good, but little else was. Donna had sold many a paper covering his debts, drugs, bi-sexual wife, messy court battles, tabloid exposes, etc.

I whispered to them, "I heard Hope's count has blue blood, but the family has been chateau rich and cash poor since before World War I."

"Yeah, they're broke," Donna said, shooing off a couple waiters who were crowding us. "I've seen the family palais. The roof leaks right over the ancient embroidered tapestries."

Genevieve appraised the Continental couple. "Both of them think they are marrying money," she said.

"Both of them are wrong," Donna stated flatly. "Hope never made good on her promise to renovate Versailles. But if enough people think she's about to marry a Count, who must have money, she can play the Island game indefinitely."

"Especially when Palm Beach hears the Crisis Center is naming itself for her. As Connie Favre always says, 'Appearances must be maintained.'"

Donna scanned the room, checking out the talent. "Brenda Ecklund is putting in an appearance. She's never looked better."

In fact, Mrs. Ecklund had firmed up and was gleaming in her orange satin gown with diamond and citrine tiara, with necklace of mandarin garnets. Her elderly husband beamed.

"What's with the tiara?" I asked. This had to be the first Palm Beach Crisis Center function where a royal crown had been donned. The only royal crown we ever saw was the cola that came from a dusty vending machine. "Except for Hope, no one else is wearing a tiara."

Donna said, "Tonight is the Vision Society's Eye Ball. Brenda will be attending after she makes the rounds here. Hope and Pierre, her Parisian paramour, will be going too."

You'd think with the murder of a notorious Tabloid Troglodyte, by an upscale former ex-shrink who was a pillar of the non-profit community, the isle of Palm Beach would be rocked to its pink coral foundations. Sworn to reform its evil ways. Nope. Nothing much changes on the world's richest island where the society circuit stays the same.

Franklin Harold got everyone's attention by tapping on a crystal goblet with a sterling fork.

"Tonight I have the pleasure of honoring one of the Island's most gracious benefactors."

He smiled at Hope. She gave a curt nod. Her dominatrix hair and scarlet lips were as stiff as ever. But her shimmering ballgown was beautiful, damn it.

"But first, I would like to announce how the Hope Louis Crisis Center of Palm Beach plans to better serve the Island. Thanks to Mrs. Louis, Dr. Mike Lavelle will be offering Support Groups for the Wealthy on a daily basis, instead of just once a week."

The attendees, most of whom wore the glittering Proud Peacocks of Palm Beach, cheered.

Harold continued, "Dr. Mike has shown such sensitivity in serving this special and misunderstood population that the Hope Louis Crisis Center is going to create a new Clinical Services department focusing on the Island. We are promoting Dr. Mike to be the division head."

More applause.

"Isn't he the one that double crossed Pete?" Genevieve asked.

"Yep and for that I will always be grateful," I said.

"I only wish I could write everything I know," Donna waved off another obsequious waiter. "But Jim and Barbara Guthrie would never recover."

After Pete persuaded the police to take him to the main psychiatric ward in West Palm Beach, he used his one phone call to try to bribe Dr. Mike to help him evade arrest.

"What you heard is true, Genevieve. Pete asked Mike to 'Baker Act' him."

"That's got to be a first," Donna laughed.

"Baker Acting" was the Florida term for taking a nut case directly to a mental health facility for evaluation, instead of turning him over to the cops. Most people who are Baker Acted are committed against their will, but Pete knew exactly what he was doing.

I explained, "Pete asked Dr. Mike to sign him in for 24 hours, but tell the authorities he would be there for the maximum 72 hours. Pete figured that would be enough time for Connie to get the plane tickets and cash for their escape to Martinique, with Dr. Mike escorting him out of the unit a day early."

"Sounds like a plan," Donna said.

"The only hitch was the admitting nurse at 45th Street recognized Pete as soon as he was brought in because he had fired her when she worked at the Crisis Center. I was the first person she called when she saw Dr. Mike's signature on Pete's admitting papers."

"What did you do next?" Genevieve said.

"As soon as I heard, I called Dr. Mike at 3:00 a.m. and told him how Pete had killed Vincent Louis and then tried to get rid of me."

"How'd he take it?"

"He was appalled. Catering to Ladies Who Lunch with a therapy chaser is one thing, but murder is another," I said. "Dr. Mike committed Pete for another two days and prescribed strong tranquilizers. He also 'forgot' to tell Connie to pack her bags."

Then Dr. Mike combed Pete's paperwork, kept in a special personnel safe at the Crisis Center, and discovered that only Pete and Connie had deluxe health insurance that would pay for medical and psychiatric treatment for up to six months. Any other staffer with the usual sparse Palm Beach Crisis Center benefits would be kicked to the curb after a couple days.

"On the second day, Dr. Mike gave me a choice: let Pete rot in the loony bin for half a year before the cops got him, or cart him off now."

"Wow? How long did it take you to decide?" Donna asked.

"A couple minutes. I did lean toward the 180-day enforced 'cure.' But then I thought Pete would corrupt the other inmates, who are only a harm to themselves."

"So you saved the mental patients of 45th Street from Pete's bad influence?" said Tom Kardos. He had just arrived and was looking snazzy in a suit and tie with little iguanas. I'd have to work on his sartorial sense.

"Great dress," he said approvingly, showing he had some sense.

"Thanks," I smiled.

Mr. Harold made another announcement. "We want to share other miracles with you on this wonderful night. You may remember the Crisis Center came under attack during that unfortunate incident when it paid for most of our executive director's legal expenses."

"But time has proven we were right to keep the faith," Harold said. "It is my honor to announce that Prison Rehab Inc. will pay the Hope Louis Crisis Center a half million a year for three years to counsel prisoners throughout the state. For this arrangement, we have none other to thank, than Peter Pignatelli."

There was a shocked gasp, but the crowd was so well lubricated at this point, I'm not sure the meaning sank in. Even Hope looked puzzled, but she applauded when everyone else did.

"How does Pete do it?" Donna asked. She whipped out her notepad. "If it were anyone else, he'd be somebody's girlfriend at the state pen right now."

I said, "Pete is way too slick for such an ordinary jailhouse fate. He has convinced himself and more importantly, Prison Ministries and a bunch of Salvation Army types who are desperate to believe in the essential goodness of man—that he is a latter day Joseph."

"Joseph from the Bible?" Tom laughed. "You've got to be kidding."

"Believe it. Pete says he is like Joseph, who was stripped, beaten and sold by his brothers into slavery in Egypt. And now when Pete does favors for the warden, it's like when Joseph advised the Pharaoh."

"The warden fell for that?" Tom asked.

"He eats it up," I said. "Pete has gotten various government and church grants for the prisoners at Stark. He also teaches mental hygiene to his fellow inmates, is a liaison with a Prisoners' Advocacy group out of Tallahassee and is in good with the prison chaplain."

"So he's really earned his special treatment," Tom said, shaking his head. He was probably remembering Pete holding me face down in the mud with a gun at my neck. Not to mention what he did to the Tabloid King.

Franklin Harold continued, "Through the efforts of Peter Pignatelli, the Hope Louis Crisis Center will improve conditions for jailbirds, ah, that is, for correctional facilities, statewide."

Donna said. "Don't tell me; I see where this is going."

"Me too," Tom said, "Pignatelli will be sprung early for good behavior . . ."

"And he will then position himself for a lucrative consulting career . . ."

"Specializing in criminal rehabilitation," Tom said. "I bet he'll make more after he gets out, than he made at the Crisis Center."

"You're good, Tom," Donna said. "Keep this up and you can be the *Shiny Sheet*'s prison correspondent."

"And I can ghost write the self help book Pete will flog once he's out," I said. "In the Belly of the Feast."

Donna nudged me. "Did you know Susan visits him every month? She brings him gourmet delicacies you can only find in Palm Beach." She glanced at Susan who was standing next to her former romantic rival, Connie Favre. Connie had been canned but was keeping up appearances.

"Felicia came out of this OK," Genevieve said. We admired her in a fitted, pink Zac Posen confection with a million tucks and tiny seams crisscrossing her bodice and narrow waistline.

"Where did Felicia get that dress?" Donna asked.

"Her mother, who else?" I said. "It was a 'welcome back' gift, when Felicia was released from the county stockade. That was after Felicia's father had taken over the Palm Beach Crisis Center when Peter was sent to jail."

"Franklin Harold doesn't need to work; why bother with the Crisis Center?" Tom asked.

"He wants his klepto daughter to have gainful employment and keep an eye on her," I answered.

At first Felicia was furious that I had told the cops the '86 Toyota Tercel had been sold from Manny's garage on 10th Avenue in Lake Worth. They deported her Latin Lover to face charges in Caracas. But then it came out that Manny had been diverting money to his model/waitress girlfriend in South Beach. Felicia stopped resenting me and we still speak although I try not to praise her wardrobe as much.

"I've seen this on the Island before," Donna said. "Felicia is one of those people who is so well connected she cannot fail. While some people battle a glass ceiling, Felicia is held up by a glass floor."

"A thick, bulletproof glass floor," I said.

Felicia's parents made a hefty contribution to the Palm Beach Crisis Center, so it would continue to employ her, but her parents set some strict ground rules. Felicia chauffeurs the elderly to doctors' offices and grocery stores in a very nice, donated car. She is not let anywhere near a Crisis Center computer, nor our books, nor does she handle donations. She is not allowed into any client's home. Her father searches her trunk every night before she leaves the office.

"That sounds like a good job for Connie," Tom said. "What's she up to?"

I answered, "Maintaining appearances. She's distanced herself from Pete and has carpeted the county with her resume, her specialty being 'women's empowerment in a culturally diverse world.'"

Tom snickered. He glanced at Connie who was being very solicitous of the oldest, most decrepit members of the Combined Charities board, who just happen to have the most money.

"You say 'women's empowerment,' but I say 'meal ticket,'" he said.

"You mean 'male ticket?'" We watched as the zaftig Connie charmed an elderly gent in a wheel chair with lavish servile attention and lilting French accent. She was good. Although these days with Viagra, gold digging isn't what it used to be.

Donna said, "Connie isn't the first to come to the Island for a marriage of convalescence."

She looked at me. "The most bizarre thing to come out of this whole Vincent Louis mess is that you still have a job. I never thought they'd let you continue working there after you turned in Peter Pignatelli and embarrassed the agency."

"No one is more shocked than me," I said, knowing the Island is not kind to whistle blowers. "And I have you to thank."

The Crew Without a Clue would have canned me right away, except I let it drop that I was friends with Donna and she would make them look bad. My grace period was about up, the Crew and the Rogue's Gallery had to wait until Hope Louis issued her reward for cracking the Vincent Louis case.

I smiled at Tom as he rolled his eyes at Hope, who proprietarily stroked the silken arm of her count. His chest was draped in a wide red sash with golden starburst medals. They gleamed under the flash from Andy Paulsen's camera and strobe light as did Hope's Proud Peacock of Palm Beach. Judging by the glittering gems, I'd say she'd given at least $400,000 to area charities.

Hope had tried to weasel out of giving her promised $1 million reward. Because Pete claimed he was not in his right mind when he killed the Tabloid King, meaning he wasn't really guilty, her lawyers argued she was not obligated. Hope would have gotten away with it too, except that Donna ran a page one column in the *Shiny Sheet*, urging Hope to pay the reward and naming Dr. Mike Lavelle and I as the recipients.

She sternly wrote, "With this shocking lapse over a technicality coming so soon after a $10 million pledge was withdrawn, one would be forced to wonder if there were any financial difficulties preventing Mrs. Louis from honoring her commitments."

That was all it took. By then, Hope knew the games Vincent had been playing to stave off bankruptcy, but if she didn't pay the reward, rumors would swirl. And those were rumors she did not want to reach her marriageable French count.

So Hope gave in, up to a point. She decided that $100,000 would be divided thus: a $10,000 peace offering to Donna (who would donate it to the cat sanctuary), $25,000 to Dr. Mike Lavelle (who got his juicy cash bonus after all) and the remainder to me.

Tonight Hope was gracing us with her first, last and only Crisis Center gala so that the entire Island would see her generosity. The socialite stood radiant before sullen waiters and the Eiffel Towerette as my pal Andy and the other society photographers raised their cameras in anticipation of capturing her good will gesture.

Then Hope Baylor Louis, resplendent in strapless, silver brocade Carolina Herrera, regally handed me the check. Ever so careful not to touch my hand, she hissed:

"Sixty-five thousand dollars is a lot of money for someone like you."

THE END

A preview of

RED, WHITE & ROYAL BLUE:

Chapter 1

CHARMED LIFE

(Washington, D. C. 1998)

Dan Bailey's staff said he was "insightful." They frequently told him he was "fascinating" and a "great judge of character."

He wasn't fooled. As the editor-in-chief at the *Washington Mirror* he wouldn't assign them good stories or put them on the front page, unless they piled it on. Bailey put it this way, "My reporters can flip the President the bird, as long as they know who is boss."

Bailey started breaking them in at the job interview. He never stood up as the supplicants entered his office; even though the girl who had just strutted in, great body and bleached hair, was probably worth it.

"Dan Bailey," he boomed, always aware of his magnetism and forceful presence. "Nice to meet you. Sit down."

The pretty woman didn't flinch as he openly stared at her chest. Bailey was surprised that they looked real. As she settled in her chair, she leaned over to give him a closer look.

"Rebecca Sharp," she said and handed Bailey a resume that would have made Janet Cooke cry. She was a Vassar graduate and fluent in French, but so was Bailey and only Nick von Hoffman knew his accent stank.

Sharp wrote for the weekly newsmagazine *7 Days* and wanted to move up by writing features at the *Washington Mirror*. Bailey's ex-wife Penelope used to be the paper's star reporter. To no one's surprise, her job and marriage terminated simultaneously. It wasn't that long ago that Bailey had announced he wanted a divorce.

"Mr. Bailey, your office is so impressive," Sharp said. She admired the wall that was solid with framed Pulitzers. She didn't know they were copies and that the publisher, Patricia Stein, kept the originals in her regal office suite upstairs.

Bailey settled into his leather executive chair, put his feet up on his mahogany desk and crossed his arms behind his head. All he lacked was a smoke. "Tell me about yourself," he commanded in his gruff, yet charming, way. She had barely started when he interrupted. That was Bailey's first step in employee training, urging his staff to cut to the chase.

He lit a cigar and stared her right in the eyes. "If you join my stable, you must combine the best of *Spy, Page Six, Manhattan, Inc., Esquire, New York* magazine and *The New York Times Sunday Magazine*. You have to be sassy, irreverent, perceptive and controversial."

Sharp blinked.

"It helps if you're clairvoyant." Bailey didn't crack a smile. "My job is to have the vision. It's up to you to work out the details."

She nodded.

Bailey was the only one in the building allowed to smoke. He didn't ask her if she minded. As the room filled with smoke, he said, "Whatever you do, don't ever bore me. Don't ever make me say, 'My eyes glaze over.'"

Becky Sharp revived his interest with a jiggle or two. She said, "I understand before you took over, the *Mirror* had never won a Pulitzer."

"That's true," he said, "I've won more awards than I can count."

"Mr. Bailey, I look forward to seeing you win the 'Brennan' award tonight," she said.

The Thomas Jefferson Center for the Protection of Free Expression was honoring the *Washington Mirror* editor as this year's champion of press freedom. Usually Bailey didn't give a rat's ass about such an obscure prize. But now it mattered. It was no Pulitzer for toppling a president, but he hoped it would make people forget the *Washington Patrician* disaster.

Sharp said, "I understand when you arrived in '64, the *Mirror* was the worst paper in the city and the *Washington Star* ruled. How times have changed."

"When I got here, taxi cabs covered more of the city than the *Mirror*," Bailey said.

She laughed.

"The staff was deadwood, the assistant metro editor was 82. I had to ease them out. Many people threatened to kill themselves."

He stopped at saying, "Those were the good old days."

Sharp blanched.

"But Bob McNamara told me there are a lot of empty threats during layoffs. One guy tried, but he botched it."

Bailey didn't tell her that he once fired a young feature writer, with stellar Ivy League credentials, for plagiarizing John Updike. A year later she slit her wrists.

Follow the author at Amazon.com/author/sharongeltner
and be the first to order *Red, White & Royal Blue*:
Washington thriller and historical novel.

ACKNOWLEDGMENTS

I am grateful to my friends and family for their unwavering encouragement and support while I wrote this book and others. I have been very lucky to benefit from their literary and journalistic discernment and their willingness to tell it like it is. They have helped me in ways beyond the book business.

I offer special thanks to: Sheila Kahn Aubrey, Susana Barciela, Gregg E. Brickman, David Geltner, Gail Geltner, C. Lynn Grosner, Jacob Grosner, Melanie Joan Hajost, Caren Johnson, Pamela Kardos-Gordon, Sharon Koskoff, Cathy Snapp Ludwig, Miles Moore, Paulette Cooper Noble, Steve Pike, Paul and Valli Polisena, Deborah Sharp and Carol Lewis West.

I express my deep gratitude to my true blue friends, Sharon Cohen and the late Melinda MacGregor, who were there for me during the tiaraless times.

.

ABOUT THE AUTHOR

Sharon Geltner's career has spanned social work, social climbing, social media and more recently, social distancing.

She was a Washington D. C. reporter, including interning with Jack Anderson, a notorious muckraking columnist, whose exposes ran nationwide. She also wrote for celebrity authors and traveled to exotic places on assignment, including Israel, Egypt, Lapland and Singapore.

Geltner came to Boca Raton, Florida to write for the Knight Ridder Tribune News, a national newspaper chain. She was briefly a war correspondent in the Mideast. However, the So Boca battle royal began when she revealed that the town's biggest philanthropist, who claimed to be a countess, had bought her illegitimate title, from a con man.

The "countess" retaliated. She announced she would cut local charities out of her $22 million will, unless Geltner and her editor left town. This high society "banned from Boca" edict appeared as far away as Frankfurt and Paris. Geltner won a National Headliners Award for Outstanding News Reporting from the Society of Professional Journalists.

Later, she publicized nonprofits, especially social service agencies, with national coverage in the *Wall Street Journal,* NBC, MSNBC, etc. One client was a Top 10 CNN Hero, honored by the Obama White House and Oprah Winfrey, who received a free, $9 million Super Bowl ad from Microsoft. Geltner also raised money at the Four Seasons in Palm Beach, with televised fashion shows, including door prizes drummed up from the Worth Avenue Ferragamo.

Her pro bono campaigns include a Barrier-Free Park in Boynton Beach, Florida for people with disabilities and launching National Net Needs News Day, a journalism appreciation campaign.

Geltner teaches, consults and owns the award-winning, multimedia agency, Froogle PR.

Made in USA - Kendallville, IN
1181029_9780991401345
10 15 2020 0835